COOK

A year in the kitchen with Britain's favourite chefs

COOK

A year in the kitchen with Britain's favourite chefs

EDITED BY **REBECCA SEAL** PHOTOGRAPHY BY **STEVEN JOYCE**

guardianbooks

ObserverFoodMonthly

For Nicola Jeal, Matt Sefton and Carmel King.

Published by Guardian Books 2010

10 9 8 7 6 5 4 3 2 1

Foreword copyright © Nigel Slater
Introduction copyright © Jay Rayner
Month introductions and '4 good things' pieces copyright © Rebecca Seal
Food photographs copyright © Steven Joyce
All the recipes are copyright © the chefs who generously donated them

First published in Great Britain in 2010 by Guardian Books, Kings Place, 90 York Way, London N1 9GU
www.guardianbooks.co.uk

A CIP catalogue record for this book is available from the British Library

ISBN 9780852652237

Food styling, art direction and recipe testing by Steven Joyce and Rebecca Seal
Designed and typeset by Two Associates
Production by Simon Rhodes

Printed and bound in China by C&C Offset Printing Co. Ltd.

Contents

Foreword

From the start, *Observer Food Monthly* has featured the best recipes around. Whether established classics from impeccable sources or fresh ideas from upcoming young cooks, recipes have long been the backbone of the magazine. The breadth of their provenance has been extraordinary, with ideas coming from professional chefs, home cooks, food producers and celebrities. What they all have in common is that they are utterly delicious.

We all use recipes in different ways. Some of us follow them word for word, others use them purely as inspiration for their own ideas. There are others still who will go along with the writer part of the way, only to put their own signature on it as the dish takes shape. At *Food Monthly* we like to think we have always offered something for every type of cook, from the most experienced to the hopeful first-timer.

As the magazine has gone from strength to strength, it has become clear that readers need a way of storing their favourite ideas, and I am sure I am not the only one to have a bulging drawer of pages torn from the hundred or more issues of the magazine. It seemed only logical to publish the most popular recipes as a collection. So here they are, the most-asked-for recipes from the magazine's many contributors, together with many new ideas, in one neat volume. We hope you enjoy it.

Nigel Slater

Introduction

Lunchtime in my house, and I am perched on the edge of the kitchen table staring at four tightly packed shelves of cookery books. Some are glossy and untouched, others dog-eared and sauce-stained. A few could be classed as works of art that really ought to be on the coffee table in the living room to be leafed through at leisure, with nibbles at my side to sate the hunger pangs; a few are ugly and difficult to use. All of them contain pages of things that I might like to eat now, or cook for my family that evening, or prepare for that special dinner party next week. The problem is that, despite years of staring at these shelves, I still have absolutely no idea where to start. It is the greedy man's nightmare, and a common one at that: a surfeit of choice.

The book you are holding is designed to be a solution to that age-old problem. It's not a replacement for those stacks of cookbooks, all of which have served me well over the years and all of which will doubtless do so again. Instead it is a fail-safe collection, a compendium, even, of all the moods you might ever have. Sometimes when it comes to satisfying appetites what you really need is all the best ideas in one place, not overly ruled by one chef's taste, or one type of ingredient, or one form of cookery.

In short, it's a continuation of the project pursued by *Observer Food Monthly* across more than a hundred editions. We have never believed there was one type of food that was worth eating, or one chef who was better than any other. We know just how varied tastes and needs can be and we have always sought to satisfy them. We have done high-end glossy and street-food grunge. We have travelled from the knottiest corners of the British Isles, across the dark earth of Western Europe, to India, China, Vietnam and back again. We have celebrated the most intricate of restaurant food, and offered up scores of ideas for dishes that will take minutes to prepare and probably less time to eat. We have only ever had one agenda: never to have an agenda. This book is exactly the same.

What it most certainly isn't, is a scissors-and-paste job. Yes, some of the recipes have previously appeared in *OFM*. We are blessed with too rich a collection not to raid our own fatly stocked larder. But many more are completely new, as are the chefs and cooks to whom they belong. You will, of course, find ideas from familiar names. We have Giorgio Locatelli's spaghetti with anchovy and tuna, and Raymond Blanc's coq au vin. We have John Torode's (foolproof) roast duck, Gordon Ramsay's mackerel pâté and the marvellous Angela Hartnett's chocolate and vanilla semifreddo.

But there are also lots of names which may be new to you, but which you will definitely want to remember: Matt Gillan from the South Lodge Hotel in Horsham, with his simple mushroom tart recipe; Sanjay Dwivedi of London's Zaika, who gives us punchy green herb chicken skewers; Richard Bertinet, of the Bertinet Kitchen Cookery School in Bath, and his luscious oxtail in red wine recipe. We very much hope that, having met them all on these pages and cooked their food, you will want to learn more about everybody who has contributed. That's why we have included details of both their restaurants – please do go and find out how they intend their food to taste – and their own cookery books. We do think ours is a book everybody should want, but we certainly don't think it's the only cookery book anybody will ever need.

Most of all we have tried to make the recipes as varied and flexible as possible. The book is arranged month by month, with a list of seasonal ingredients, so you know what's best when, but we never have been and aren't now doctrinaire. What you decide to cook and when you cook it is entirely up to you. It just made the most sense to do it that way. You'll get no apologies from us for including some seriously complicated recipes which read less like cooking challenges and more like a special project NASA might undertake.

But then something like Pierre Koffman's marvellous braised pig trotters stuffed with morels is a true modern classic, a slice of his native Gascony, and it's always a pleasure to see it in print. It was a hit when it appeared on the menu at his London three-Michelin-starred restaurant La Tante Claire until that closed in 2004. Likewise, when he ran his pop-up version on the roof of Selfridges in 2009 – the restaurant was meant to be open for a couple of weeks but stayed there for three months due to demand – it was one of the most popular dishes. You may never have the nerve to take on the challenge, but just reading about it is a thrill. You'll also find the recipe for roasted bone marrow with parsley salad from Fergus Henderson's famed nose-to-tail-eating restaurant St John. This book wouldn't have been complete without it.

At the other end of the scale we have gloriously simple ideas, which are less recipes than riffs on ingredients: four ways with leeks, or chicken, or tofu (we are a broad church). In between there are lots of those dishes which will quickly become irresistible standbys, always ready to be pressed into service: Skye Gyngell's roasted beetroot salad, Thomasina Miers's sticky Mexican ribs, Sally Clarke's pasta with goats cheese and chives. Oh, and a gutsy pork and chorizo stew, just perfect for winter, by some baggy-arsed restaurant critic, with an overdeveloped appetite and too much hair. (Trust me. It's great. My kids adore it.)

Finally, to season the mix, look out for the trade secrets with which the text is liberally scattered: from the best saucepan to use, to the joys of certain ingredients, be it a particular kind of salt or the myriad uses for rosewater (a killer detail in any dessert, apparently). As to the photographs, we have a firm no-artificial-flavourings-or-colourings rule. No dish has had its looks photoshopped or massaged: we simply shot what came out of the oven or the pan or the bowl. So if you think it looks delicious, there's really only one reason. Because it is.

Sure, it's pretty. *OFM* has always recognised the importance of the visual and it makes sense that this book should look good too. But we know that looks aren't everything. What really matters is how things taste, and we think what's in here will taste terrific. Though please, whatever you do, don't treat it as some kind of holy scripture handed down from on high. The very best cookery books are not examinations to be passed or failed. They are a conversation between the cook and the page, between appetite and ingredient, between emotion and effort. That conversation has been at the heart of everything we have ever wanted to do at *OFM*, and we're thrilled that it's at the heart of this book too. So start turning the pages and thinking about your next meal. You never know where that journey will take you.

Jay Rayner

A short note about the text

Weights and measures

All measures in this book are metric. The following is a rough guide if you prefer to work in imperial.

1 ounce = 28g
1 pound = 450g
1 pint   = 570ml

Temperatures

The following is only a guide. Check your oven manual for exact conversions as ovens can vary.

110°C = 225°F = gas ¼   190°C = 375°F = gas 5
130°C = 250°F = gas ½   200°C = 400°F = gas 6
140°C = 275°F = gas 1   220°C = 425°F = gas 7
150°C = 300°F = gas 2   230°C = 450°F = gas 8
170°C = 325°F = gas 3   240°C = 475°F = gas 9
180°C = 350°F = gas 4

Remember, if you are cooking with a fan oven, you will probably need to lower the temperature by approximately 20°C or 40°F, and reduce the overall cooking time by 10 minutes for every hour.

Food safety

Several of the recipes in this book contain raw or lightly cooked eggs – for these, it is best to use very fresh, free-range organic eggs.

Ingredients

Recipes in this book make extensive use of locally produced ingredients, although there are inevitably exceptions. Some ingredients are seasonal and so subject to the vagaries of the weather. We have noted when they are usually available, but this can change from year to year.

January

Beetroot, Brussels sprouts, cauliflower, celeriac, celery, chicory, Jerusalem artichokes, kale, leeks, mushrooms, parsnips, potatoes, swede, turnips, Seville oranges; guinea fowl, hare, partridge, venison; and brill, clams, cockles, haddock, halibut and hake are all good this month.

January is a month for warming food – meaty roasts, hearty suppers and indulgent puddings. Forget about dieting until the weather brightens; this month should be all about making yourself feel good with Rowley Leigh's delicious roast potatoes, Eric Chavot's quick fish pie and Shaun Hill's steamed orange pudding.

Mitch Tonks

Mitch Tonks is a self-taught chef and fishmonger. He founded the FishWorks chain and has been hailed as, among other good things, the new Rick Stein. He has two excellent restaurants, the Seahorse Seafood and Meat Grill in Dartmouth, and RockFish Grill and Seafood Market in Bristol. This recipe is from *Fish*. He's also published a number of other books, including *The Fishmonger's Cookbook*.

Hake with parsley and creamed kale

Kale reminds me of a sea vegetable and I think its fairly strong flavour works perfectly with most fish, especially the soft, slightly sweet flavour of hake. Kale is also very good eaten raw or tossed with capers, finely chopped onion and lemon juice and served with a fatty fish such as salmon. Ask your fishmonger for fillets of hake, preferably from a larger fish of around 2kg.

serves 2
½ onion
2 bay leaves
6 cloves
500ml milk
350g kale
vegetable oil for frying
2 x 180g hake fillets

salt and pepper
40g butter
40g flour
75ml double cream
1 tsp finely chopped capers
a small handful of finely chopped parsley
squeeze of lemon

Preheat the oven to maximum. Prepare the white sauce for the kale by making 2 cuts into the onion and inserting the bay leaves into them, then sticking the cloves into the onion. Pour the milk into a saucepan, add the onion and bring to a gentle simmer for 4–5 minutes. Then turn the heat off, allow to infuse for about half an hour, and remove the onion.

Cook the kale for about 10 minutes in plenty of boiling salted water, then drain.

Heat some oil in a frying pan and when just starting to smoke, lightly season the hake fillets with salt and pepper on the skin side and lay them in the pan, skin-side down, and cook for 4–5 minutes until the skin is crispy and golden. Carefully turn the fish over and place the pan in the oven (making sure it is suitable for the oven; if not, put the fish on a roasting tray) and cook for a further 3–4 minutes.

In another pan, melt the butter and stir in the flour until you have a creamy paste, which is known as a roux. Slowly add the milk and cream to the roux while continually stirring over a gentle heat. Your sauce should be just thicker than double cream. Then add the kale, cream, capers and parsley, taste and season and add just a squeeze of lemon juice. Divide the creamed kale onto two plates and put the cooked fish on top.

Rowley Leigh

Rowley Leigh tried farming and novel-writing before turning to cooking, and is now one of the most influential chefs in Britain. He's well known for the food he served at Kensington Place in the 1990s, and in 2007 he opened the equally successful restaurant Le Café Anglais in Bayswater, London. He is a much-loved cookery writer and the author of *No Place Like Home*.

Perfect roast potatoes

I have roasted potatoes in olive oil, sunflower oil, chicken fat, beef dripping, pork fat and goose fat, all with beneficial results. I tend to use the fat from whatever joint I happen to be cooking, augmented by sunflower oil. The most important tip is that the potatoes should not be 'parboiled' but pretty well cooked – this takes a certain nerve, as they can fall apart if overcooked. If they do, don't worry but carry on anyway – the result will still be good. The flour-and-mustard trick helps to give a crisp coating.

serves 2
2kg large floury potatoes
sea salt
4 tbs plain flour
1 tbs mustard powder
250ml oil or fat

Peel the potatoes and cut them into small pieces the size of a large walnut. Rinse well before placing in a large saucepan and covering in cold water. Add 1 tsp salt, bring to the boil and simmer gently until the potatoes are just on the point of being cooked.

Drain the potatoes in a colander and sprinkle over the flour and mustard powder, tossing the potatoes as you do so to ensure they are evenly coated. Heat an oven tray with the oil or fat and carefully slide in the potatoes, spreading them evenly over the surface. Do not attempt to turn them or roll them in the oil but simply leave them to roast for 20 minutes at 220°C/gas 7. Once they have a rich golden crust on the bottom, the potatoes can be turned and allowed to brown for a further 20 minutes. Drain again in a colander and sprinkle with sea salt. Serve as soon as possible.

Maldon sea salt tastes completely different from all other salts. It has a far superior flavour. I love the way it looks and feels and how it explodes on your tongue. I cannot imagine life without it.

Tom Norrington-Davies
Fettuccine with roasted mushrooms

Roast 4 large field mushrooms with a generous slug of olive oil and a pinch of sea salt. They will take about 15–20 minutes. Once they are done, slice them roughly and toss them with 2 tbs olive oil, a chopped clove of garlic, a small bunch of chopped parsley, and the grated zest and the squeezed juice of half a lemon. Boil enough fettuccine or tagliatelle for 2 people and, once it is cooked and drained, toss it with the marinated mushrooms. Season to your liking and serve garnished with plenty of grated Parmesan.

Hugh Fearnley-Whittingstall
Roast leg of hogget

Take a leg of hogget or mutton. Chop together a fistful of parsley, 2 cloves of garlic, about 6 anchovies, and 1 tbs capers. Make incisions deep into the meat with a sharp knife, and push in ½ tsp of the mixture. Roast for 45 minutes at 220°C/ gas 7, then pour over a glass of white wine and a glass of water. Turn down to 180°C/ gas 4 and roast for another 45–75 minutes, depending on the size of the joint and how pink you like your meat. Rest the joint for at least 20 minutes before carving, while you make gravy from the winey juices in the pan.

Thomasina Miers
Welsh rarebit

Thinly slice or grate 100g mature cheddar (or preferably Lincolnshire Poacher). Put 30g butter and 1 tsp flour in a small saucepan and cook for a few minutes. Add 70ml dark ale, salt and pepper and the cheese. Cook over a low heat until the cheese has melted. Do not allow to get too hot. Pour over a piece of toast and put under the grill for a minute. Dust with cayenne or sprinkle with Worcestershire sauce and eat at once.

Eric Chavot
Smash fish pie

It is very easy to make a really fast fish pie. First, turn the oven on full. Then get a piece of smoked haddock and poach it for 2–3 minutes covered in milk, with a bay leaf and a little olive oil. When the fish is cooked, grab a packet of instant mash, but rather than using water, make it with the poaching milk instead. Microwave some frozen peas. Flake the fish. Put it in an ovenproof dish with the peas, then cover it with the mash and a sprinkling of cheese. Brown it in the hot oven. You can add a little butter to the mash if you prefer it a bit richer – without it then this is really pretty healthy.

Matt Gillan

Matt Gillan, 28, is already executive chef at the Pass at South Lodge Hotel in Horsham, but has had no formal training, preferring instead to learn on the job at Michelin-starred restaurants like Midsummer House in Cambridge, Gordon Ramsay at Royal Hospital Road in London and the Vineyard at Stockcross.

Mushroom tarts

makes 16 small tarts
400g block puff pastry
2 onions
1kg mixed mushrooms (button, chestnut, oyster, shitake)
3 tbs chopped chives
salt
50g Parmesan

Roll the pastry out until about ¹/₂ cm thick. Place it onto a baking tray covered with non-stick paper. Place another sheet of paper on top and then another baking tray. Bake for 15 minutes at 170°C/gas 3. Remove from oven and allow to cool. Cut into 12cm by 6cm rectangles with a serrated knife.

Peel the onions and cut in half. Very finely slice them and put them into a saucepan. Place on a moderate heat and cook until golden, stirring occasionally to avoid burning.

Cut the mushrooms into quarters. Heat a frying pan and add a little oil. Fry the mushrooms in batches to ensure they don't get too wet and their moisture is not released. Put them into a bowl to keep warm. Add the chives and a little salt and mix together.

Spread a layer of the cooked caramelised onion onto the pastry. Arrange the mushrooms on the onion and then finish with the Parmesan by using a peeler to create shavings.

Giorgio Locatelli

Giorgio Locatelli is one of the best Italian chefs working in Britain today, and his brilliant Michelin-starred restaurant, Locanda Locatelli, is very popular. In 1986 he came to Britain to work at the Savoy, followed by a stint in Paris. Back in London he was head chef at Olivo before opening Zafferano in 1995, where he also got a Michelin star. He now runs his own restaurant with his wife, Plaxy. His latest book is called *Made in Italy: Food and Stories*.

Spaghetti with anchovy and tuna

A great recipe, very tasty. This is store-cupboard cooking at its easiest, so perfect for busy parents, and children always love it.

serves 4

350g spaghetti
2 tbs olive oil
2 cloves of garlic, each cut into quarters
4 anchovy fillets in oil, drained
250g canned tuna in olive oil, drained

50ml white wine
50g capers, rinsed and drained
2 tomatoes, diced
10 basil leaves
2 tbs extra-virgin olive oil
sea salt and freshly ground black pepper

Cook the spaghetti in a large pot of boiling salted water for about 8 minutes, until al dente – tender but still firm to the bite. Meanwhile, heat the olive oil in a frying pan, add the garlic and fry over a gentle heat for 3 minutes. Add the anchovy fillets and cook very gently until almost melting. Increase the heat and add the tuna. Toss for a few minutes, then add the white wine and let it bubble for a few minutes to allow the alcohol to evaporate. Stir in the capers and tomatoes.

Drain the pasta, reserving 2–3 tbs of the cooking water. Toss the spaghetti with the sauce, mix in the basil leaves and extra-virgin olive oil and season to taste. Add a little of the cooking water if the pasta seems too dry, then serve. In Italy, you wouldn't put cheese on a pasta with any sort of seafood, even canned tuna.

I stopped buying olive oil from the supermarket. It sits on the shelves too long. Now I buy mine on the internet from a producer called Armando Manni in Seggiano, Tuscany. I use **Manni Per Me** for meaty things or **Manni Per Mio** for lighter dishes.

TRICKS OF THE TRADE

'Whether wild or cultivated, mushrooms should never be washed. Use a soft brush or slightly damp cloth to clean them. Mushrooms are already full of water, so placing them in more destroys the flavour.'

Gennaro Contaldo

Pierre Koffman

Pierre Koffman is one of the most revered chefs in the country and many other brilliant chefs have worked in his kitchens. His pop-up Restaurant on the Roof of Selfridges in 2009, five years after he'd closed the hugely popular La Tante Claire, was only meant to run for ten days, but demand for his traditional French cooking was so high that it eventually ran for over three months. This recipe is one of his most famous, taken from *Tante Claire: Recipes from a Master Chef* by Pierre Koffman and Timothy Shaw.

Stuffed pig's trotters with morels

serves 4

4 pig's back trotters
100g carrots, diced
100g onions, diced
150ml dry white wine
1 tbs port
150ml veal stock
225g veal sweetbreads, blanched and chopped

75g butter, plus a knob for the sauce
20 dried morels, soaked until soft, and drained
1 small onion, finely chopped
1 chicken breast, skinned and diced
1 egg white
200ml double cream
knob of butter, to serve
salt and freshly ground black pepper

Preheat the oven to 160°C/gas 3. Place the trotters in a casserole with the diced carrots and onions, the wine, port and veal stock. Cover and braise in the oven for 3 hours.

Meanwhile, fry the sweetbreads in the butter for 5 minutes, add the morels and chopped onion and cook for another 5 minutes. Leave to cool.

Purée the chicken breast with the egg white and cream, and season with salt and pepper. Mix with the sweetbread mixture to make the stuffing.

Take the trotters out of the casserole and strain the cooking stock, keeping the stock but discarding the vegetables. Open the trotters out flat and lay each one on a piece of foil. Leave to cool.

Fill the cooled trotters with the chicken stuffing and roll tightly in foil. Chill in the fridge for at least 2 hours.

Preheat the oven to 220°C/gas 7 or prepare a steamer, and when the water is simmering, steam the foil-wrapped trotters until heated through. Alternatively, put the trotters in a casserole, cover and heat in the oven for 15 minutes. Put the trotters on a serving dish and remove the foil. Pour the reserved stock into the casserole and reduce by half.

Whisk in a knob of butter, pour the sauce over the trotters and serve very hot.

Poilâne bread has a great flavour and I love it toasted with a good egg.

4 good things to do with broccoli

Broccoli with garlic
Break a head of broccoli into florets and cook in salted boiling water for a couple of minutes, until just tender (cook it for longer if you like it with less bite). Drain and return to the pan with a splash of olive oil or a knob of butter and a clove of garlic which you've either chopped finely or put through a crusher. Stir-fry briefly until the garlic is just slightly sizzling and fragrant. Serve with a couple of grinds of black pepper. You could toss this with some tagliatelle with the addition of a bit more decent olive oil and maybe even a crumbled dried red chilli.

Broccoli with soy sauce and chilli
Chop a red chilli into fine rings, removing or leaving in the seeds depending on your tolerance for heat. Boil the broccoli as before, until just al dente, drain and return to the pan with a little vegetable or groundnut oil and stir-fry with the chilli and a couple of generous splashes of soy sauce.

Broccoli and blue cheese soup
Chop up an onion and fry in butter or oil in a big saucepan until soft and translucent, then add a couple of large diced potatoes and two heads of broccoli, also chopped into pieces. Fry gently for a couple of minutes. Add a litre or so of stock (vegetable or chicken is fine), season with salt and pepper and cook for 20 minutes or until the potatoes are tender. You could blend it at this point, or leave it chunky. Then, stir in a couple of handfuls of crumbled blue cheese, and a dollop of cream if you like. If it's too thick, add a little more hot stock or water. Crumble a little more cheese on top at the table.

Broccoli and creamy pasta sauce
Cook enough pasta for one person and meanwhile cook a handful of broccoli florets in salted water. Drain and toss the hot broccoli and cooked pasta with at least 3 tbs double cream or crème fraiche, some freshly grated Parmesan (quite a lot), fresh black pepper, a little salt and some torn-up basil leaves.

David Jones

David Jones is from Huddersfield and is executive chef at Momo, restaurateur Mourad Mazouz's North African restaurant in London (he also owns Sketch, and bars and restaurants in Paris). Jones opened Chintamani in London's Jermyn Street in 2002 and Mourad later asked him to help open Momo in Selfridges. In 2008 he helped run the year-long pop-up restaurant the Double Club with Mourad and Prada.

Roast venison with celeriac

serves 4
500g trimmed venison loin
butter
1 tsp ras el hanout (a North African spice mix, available online and in specialist food shops)
120g chanterelle mushrooms
1 packet baby-leaf chard

for the celeriac confit:
1 small head of celeriac
250ml vegetable stock
150ml olive oil
1 sprig of rosemary
1 sprig of thyme
2 confit lemons (you can buy these, as above, or make them, see right)

For the venison jus:
1 carrot
1 onion
1 celery stick
1 leek
2 tbs olive oil
1 bulb of garlic
1 sprig of thyme
1 bay leaf
10 white peppercorns, crushed
500ml port
1½l red wine
1½l chicken stock
1½l veal stock
salt and pepper

Make the confit lemons in advance. Cut 8 lemons into quarters, but leave them attached at the base. Sprinkle with salt all over the inside and outside of the lemons. Place in a sterilised preserving jar and seal for 3–4 weeks. (These are great with chicken or even chopped tomato salad.) You may want to rinse them before use as they can be salty.

To make the celeriac confit, peel the celeriac and cut into 1.5cm thick batons. Heat all the other ingredients together in a pan and bring to the boil. Add the celeriac and boil gently for 10–12 minutes, cover with cling film and take off the heat. Leave in a warm place to cool down slowly and make a confit. If your batons are thicker than 1.5cm they will need boiling in the stock for a few minutes longer.

To make the jus, cut the vegetables into small cubes. Heat a heavy-bottomed pan, add the olive oil, vegetables, garlic, herbs and peppercorns, then caramelise. Add the port and reduce to the thickness of a glaze. Add the red wine and reduce to a glaze again. Add the chicken and veal stocks and cook on a low simmer for 35–40 minutes. Then pass through a fine sieve and reduce until it coats the back of the spoon (this will make twice as much as you need, so you could freeze half). Season to taste.

Roast the venison loin in butter at 200°C/gas 6 for 12 minutes (the meat will be rare). Then take out the venison and rest for 10 minutes. In the same pan cook off the ras el hanout for a minute or two, then add the mushrooms and cook in the pan juices and a little oil.

To plate up, slice the venison into 8, place 4 celeriac batons on each plate, then 2 thick slices of venison on top with mushrooms around. Heat the sauce and glaze the venison, then sprinkle with baby-leaf chard.

Henry Harris

Henry Harris met Simon Hopkinson while training at Leith's School of Food and Wine in London, and after travelling and working at Chez Panisse in California, worked for him at Hilaire and Bibendum. He then opened the Fifth Floor restaurant at Harvey Nichols. In 2002 he opened his own award-winning French restaurant, Racine. He has published two books, *The Harvey Nichols Fifth Floor Cookbook* and *A Passion for Protein*.

Roast woodcock or snipe with Armagnac

The most important part of this recipe is to ensure that the bird is at a comfortable room temperature before you start the cooking.

serves 2
2 woodcock or 4 snipe, plucked and most definitely with the
guts in butter
salt and pepper
2 slices of pain Poilâne (or sourdough bread)
Armagnac

Preheat the oven to 180°C/gas 4. Remove the head from each bird and use the long beak to pin the legs so they nestle just under the breastbone.

Slather the birds generously with butter and season with salt and pepper. Place them in an ovenproof frying pan and roast for 6–8 minutes for the snipe and 10–12 minutes for the woodcock. Baste halfway through the cooking process. Remove from the oven and put the birds in a dish and keep warm for ten minutes. Fry the two slices of bread in the cooking pan over a gentle heat until lightly crisped. Set to one side.

Draw the entrails from the birds and mash with a fork. Spread onto the toast and place the birds on top. Wash the pan with some Armagnac and set fire to it. Spoon over the birds and serve immediately.

Kikkoman soy sauce is the only naturally brewed soy sauce readily available, and used as a seasoning it provides another layer of flavour in the savoury department.

4 good things to do with cheddar

Cheddar tartlets
Buy some ready-made savoury tartlet pastry cases. For each one, mix an egg yolk with enough double cream to not quite fill the case and add a hefty grating of good cheddar, with a little pepper. Bake in a medium oven until everything is golden and slightly puffed up. Caramelised sliced onion would be a good addition to the filling, as would either lightly fried leeks, mushrooms, lardons or slices of cooked red pepper.

Spinach pasta bake
Cook some pasta. Make a white sauce, enough to cover the pasta. Wilt 3 or 4 large handfuls of spinach in butter. Mix this with the sauce, a generous quantity of grated cheddar and lots of black pepper – you could also add a dusting of nutmeg. Top with more cheddar. Brown under the grill.

Baked potatoes stuffed with cheese
Bake a potato (properly, not in the microwave), cut it in half, scoop out the flesh and mash roughly with a spoonful of cream cheese (something with garlic or herbs would be good) or crème fraiche and some salt and pepper. You could also mix in some finely chopped chives, leek, ham or even fried onions. Push the mash back into the skins and cover with grated cheese. Return to the oven and bake until the cheese is golden.

Tomato cheese on toast
Make cheese on toast, but smear the cheese with tomato purée before it goes under the grill. Cook until bubbling and the puree is just slightly browned.

Shaun Hill

Shaun Hill worked for Robert Carrier ('at about the time of the Battle of Hastings', as he puts it) then at Gidleigh Park in Devon, and ran the Merchant House in Ludlow, which was a place of foodie pilgrimage until he closed it in 2005. He was lured back to the kitchen when the Walnut Tree Inn, near Abergavenny, came on the market. His books include *How to Cook Better*, *Better Gravy and Other Kitchen Secrets* and *Cooking at the Merchant House*.

Steamed orange pudding

Sponge puddings that use flour with butter and baking powder rather than suet are much lighter and easier to both make and eat. A good marmalade made with the new season's Seville oranges would be fine in place of the syrup

serves 4
100g soft butter plus extra for greasing dariole moulds or ramekins
100g caster sugar
100g self-raising flour
25g fresh breadcrumbs
½ tsp baking powder
2 eggs
2 tbs milk
juice and zest of 2 oranges
4 tbs golden syrup

Cream together the soft butter and sugar. Stir in the flour, breadcrumbs and baking powder. Stir in the eggs, milk and orange zest and juice. Butter 4 dariole (small, narrow metal pudding) moulds or ramekins, then put a spoonful of golden syrup, or marmalade, or a combination of both, into each.

Pour in the batter. Place a small circle of non-stick or greaseproof paper across the top of each mould. Place in a deep roasting tray half filled with hot water, then bake at 200°C/gas 6 for 40 minutes. Then, carefully, turn out.

February

Cabbage, carrots, cauliflowers, celeriac, chard, chicory, endive, leeks, forced rhubarb, protected spinach, swede and turnips are all good this month.

Cheer up February with Vivek Singh's winter vegetable curry, or spend a lazy weekend afternoon making Mark Hix's mutton hotpot. Get some friends round for Giuseppe Turi's pork shoulder in milk, or do a roast with some creamy leeks.

Shaun Hill

Twice-baked goat's cheese soufflé

makes 20
700ml whole milk
100g unsalted butter, softened
100g plain flour
8 egg yolks
12g cornflour
12 egg whites, whisked until stiff
500g goat's cheese, crumbled
1 tbs English mustard
1 tbs Worcestershire sauce
a dash of Tabasco
salt and pepper

Heat the milk. Make a beurre manié by mixing the softened butter with the flour very thoroughly, using your hands. Then whisk into the hot milk to thicken. Bring to the boil. Remove from the heat then beat in the egg yolks and cornflour.

Fold in the egg whites, then all the other ingredients. Spoon the mixture into 20 greased ramekins. Place in a deep roasting tray. Fill the tray to halfway with hot water, then bake at 180°C/gas 4 until risen – about 15 minutes. You can then remove them from the oven and keep the soufflés in the fridge until you want to serve them. When you are ready, bake again until golden for about 25 minutes.

I *always* keep a bottle of green Tabasco in the cupboard.

Tim Hughes

Tim Hughes is chef-director of the Caprice Restaurant Group and looks after the group's 30 sites and their restaurants, including the Ivy, J Sheekey, Scott's and the Rivington restaurants. Born in Hove, he started his career on a Youth Training Scheme at Chatsworth Hotel, then worked in Switzerland before returning to the UK to work in several famous restaurants, including Harvey's under Marco Pierre White.

Le Caprice's steak tartare

Steak tartare has been on the menu at Le Caprice since 1981.

serves 4
500g very fresh lean fillet, sirloin or topside steak, minced
3 shallots, peeled and finely chopped
2 tbs chopped capers
a few dashes of brandy
1 tbs tomato ketchup
2–3 tsp Worcestershire sauce
a few dashes Tabasco or more if you wish
1 tbs olive oil
salt and pepper

Ask your butcher to mince the meat through a clean mincer or, better still, do it yourself if you have a mincer attachment for your mixing machine.

Mix all the ingredients together and check the seasoning – you may wish to add a little more Tabasco, ketchup or Worcestershire sauce. Spoon the steak tartare on to a plate, or if you prefer, push it into a ramekin to mould, then turn it out onto a plate to serve. Serve with fine-cut chips, green salad or toast.

Shane Osborn

Shane Osborn was born in Perth and was the first Australian chef ever to get a Michelin star. His elegant modern-European food has won lots of awards, including Readers' Choice at the World's 50 Best Restaurants Awards in 2007. He has worked for Tom Aikens, Marcus Wareing and Gordon Ramsay, and is now head chef and co-owner of the two-starred Pied à Terre in London's Charlotte Street. His book is called *Starters*.

Soft polenta with Gruyère and mushroom fricassée
Polenta is also a fantastic accompaniment to veal dishes and steaks.

serves 4
500ml chicken stock or vegetable stock
salt
200g polenta
2 tbs extra-virgin olive oil
2 cloves of garlic, peeled
150g wild mushrooms
black pepper
1 sprig of parsley, picked and chopped
½ a lemon
120g Gruyère cheese, grated
3 tbs unsalted butter

In a large saucepan bring the stock to the boil. Add a pinch of salt and then slowly pour in the polenta flour, whisking continuously to ensure there are no lumps. Cook, stirring frequently, for about 15–20 minutes or until the flour has absorbed the stock and no longer tastes mealy.

In a medium-sized frying pan heat the olive oil, then add the garlic and when it starts to smoke, add the mushrooms and season them immediately. Cook for 2–3 minutes, add the parsley and a squeeze of lemon. Tip out onto a plate, cover and keep warm. Once the polenta is cooked, fold in 100g of the cheese and the butter, and then season. Arrange the polenta in the centre of 4 hot plates and top with the mushroom fricassée, then garnish with the remaining 20g of grated cheese.

Shane Osborn

Sweet potato and goat's cheese terrine

serves 8–10
2 large sweet potatoes
olive oil
450g goat's cheese, softened
1 tsp Italian parsley, chopped
1 tsp chives, chopped
1 tsp marjoram, chopped
salt and freshly ground black pepper, to taste

Peel the sweet potatoes and cut them lengthwise into 2mm slices. Cook the sweet potatoes in olive oil in a large sauté pan for 6–8 minutes over a medium-high heat, until they are cooked but have not gained any colour. Place them on paper towels to cool and set aside for now. In a bowl, combine all the other ingredients, mixing thoroughly.

Line a small loaf tin with cling film, ensuring that the plastic wrap is pushed into the corners. (This will give your terrine sharp edges, not rounded.) Trim the sweet potato slices so that they will fit in the bottom of the tin, using just enough to cover the bottom. Line the bottom with sweet potato and layer with about 2cm of herbed cheese. Layer more sweet potato slices on top of the goat's cheese. Continue this process until the tin is full, finishing with a layer of sweet potato. Fold the plastic wrap over the top and chill until set. Turn out, slice and serve with rocket and a little salad dressing.

Tom Norrington Davies
Chicken with noodles

Grill 2 free-range chicken breasts and, once they are done, slice them thinly and toss the slices with 2 cloves of chopped garlic, a small bunch of chopped coriander, the juice and zest of a small lime and 2 tsps sesame oil. Season with salt and a pinch of crushed dried chillies. Boil 2 nests of noodles and toss them with the chicken.

John Torode
Steamed roast chicken

Season the outside of your bird and pour half a cup of water into the cavity. The chicken will steam from the inside, so you should be able to cook it in 75 minutes at 200°C/gas 6, and it won't dry out. Lovely.

Mitch Tonks
Herb-stuffed fish supper

Slash a sea bass or sea bream, weighing about 450g, a couple of times, stuff it with rosemary, thyme or fresh bay leaves, rub with olive oil and roast for 20 minutes in a hot oven.

Atul Kochhar
Perfect rice

Use a 1:1 ratio of rice to water, called the pilau method, so if you're cooking a kilo of rice use a litre of water. First, sauté a few cardamon pods, a few cloves and a chopped onion in a little butter and add a good dollop of yoghurt. Then sauté the rice in a little butter and oil for a minute or two. Add the water and bring it all to the boil. When you can see the top of the rice emerging from the water, cover the pan tightly with a cloth and then put a tight-fitting lid on top. You can either put the pan into a low oven for 10 minutes, or leave it on a very low heat on the hob. Finally leave it, covered, for about 15 minutes, off the heat.

Vivek Singh

Vivek Singh started his career making in-flight meals in Mumbai, but quickly worked his way up to a position in the Grand Hotel in Calcutta and then the Rajvilas Hotel in Jaipur. In 2001 he co-founded the Cinnamon Club in London with Iqbal Wahhab and in 2008 he opened the Cinnamon Kitchen (which won Best New Restaurant at the British Curry Awards 2009) and published his third and most comprehensive book – *Curry: Classic and Contemporary*.

Winter vegetable curry with carrots, peas and tomatoes (Gajjar mutter tamatar ki subzi)

This humble vegetable curry is cooked in almost every household in northern India. Generally considered too mundane to put on restaurant menus, it is an all-time favourite at home, and comes in many guises – made with cauliflower or turnips, or served with lots of sauce. If the water is omitted, this semi-dry dish goes down a treat with chapattis. I rather prefer the drier version, as the flavours are more pronounced.

serves 4
3 tbs vegetable or corn oil
1 bay leaf
4 green cardamom pods
1 tsp cumin seeds
3 onions, finely chopped
3 ripe tomatoes, blended to a purée
2.5cm piece of fresh ginger, finely chopped
2 green chillies, cut lengthwise in half

½ tsp ground turmeric
½ tsp red chilli powder
1 tsp ground cumin
1 tsp ground coriander
2 tsp salt
4 carrots, peeled and cut into 1cm dice
200g peas
250ml water
juice of 1 lemon
2 tbs chopped fresh coriander or dill

Heat the oil in a heavy-based pan, add the bay leaf, cardamom pods and cumin seeds and let them crackle. Add the chopped onions and cook over a fairly high heat until golden brown. Stir in the puréed tomatoes, ginger, green chillies, spices and salt and cook for 8–10 minutes, until the oil begins to separate from the mixture at the sides of the pan. Add the carrots and cook, stirring, for 2 minutes, then add the peas and cook for 3 minutes. Pour in the water and cook till the vegetables are tender but still retain a little bite. Check the seasoning, then stir in the lemon juice and sprinkle with the chopped herbs. Serve hot with with chapattis or naan bread.

Tip: if you cut the carrots even smaller, in 5mm dice, and cook the mixture without adding any water, then it can be used as a topping for canapés or as a filling for wraps (made using supermarket tortillas, if you like). Papdi – wheat crisps, available in Indian supermarkets – topped with this vegetable curry make a good canapé.

Giuseppe Turi

Giuseppe Turi is originally from Puglia and came to London in 1982, where he joined the Athenæum Hotel as sommelier. He went on to work at the Connaught Hotel in 1985 and later became maître d'. He returned to the Athenæum in 1987 as restaurant manager, and left to open Enoteca Turi in 1990, which he runs with his wife Pamela. Although it's been open for 20 years the restaurant still constantly wins awards.

Pork shoulder roasted in milk

serves 6
1 large onion
100g butter
100ml olive oil
5 cloves of garlic, crushed
2 sprigs of sage
2 sprigs of rosemary
4 bay leaves
1.2 kg deboned pork shoulder
150ml white wine
800ml whole milk

Coarsely chop the onion. Put 50g of the butter and 50ml of the olive oil, the chopped onion and crushed garlic, sage, rosemary and bay leaves in a frying pan and sauté until golden brown. In another frying pan, with the remainder of the olive oil and butter, brown the meat on all sides.

Put the vegetables and meat into a large casserole dish, and add the white wine and milk. Bake in the oven at 220°C/gas 7 for half an hour. Turn down the heat to 160°C/gas 2 and cook for a further 2 hours. Keep checking the liquid every half hour. Add a little water if necessary – you need to end up with 250ml of sauce.

Take out of the oven, and remove the pork from the dish. Cover with foil and let it rest on a chopping board. Sieve the juice into a saucepan, using a coarse sieve. Squeeze all the juice out of the vegetables and skim off some of the fat if you wish. Season and reheat the sauce. Slice the pork and serve, pouring the sauce over the meat, with some braised Savoy cabbage and celeriac and potato mash.

Prestige

4 good things to do with roast chicken

Lemon and thyme

Cut an unwaxed lemon into quarters and chuck it into the cavity of the chicken. Throw in some whole peeled cloves of garlic and a handful of lemon thyme sprigs. Roast as normal. Afterwards deglaze the pan with white wine or stock and perhaps a splash of cream for a light lemony sauce. Use a little flour to thicken if you like.

Smoked paprika and coriander

Mix 5 tbs olive oil with a crushed clove of garlic, 1 tsp smoked paprika, a large handful of roughly chopped coriander, salt and pepper, and rub it all over the chicken (you could also push it under the skin, see right, which will stop the leaves and garlic from charring). Make short incisions in the thighs to let the spices (and the heat) penetrate the meat. You could also include chilli flakes. Halve an onion and pop it into the cavity. Roast as normal, basting occasionally with the red smoky juices. You can serve slivers of the cooked onion as an accompaniment. Serve with yoghurt mixed with cucumber, garlic and/or fresh coriander and mint.

Herby crispy skin

Gently pull back the skin of the chicken around the cavity and slide your hands between it and the breast meat, loosening the skin. Mix 50g butter with a handful of roughly chopped thyme, rosemary, or marjoram and parsley, plus some salt and pepper and some chopped garlic, if you like. Push the butter under the skin of the chicken. Lay three pieces of smoked streaky bacon over the breast. Roast as normal, basting with the buttery herby juices.

Onion

Roast the chicken on a layer of halved onions, which will cook down to a caramelised squidge. About three quarters of an hour before it's done, add big chunks of almost-cooked boiled potato to the roasting dish and baste them with the oniony juices (you may need to add a little more fat – vegetable oil or goose fat are good – which should be allowed to get hot before the potatoes go in).

TRICKS OF THE TRADE

'When using parsley in soups, stocks and stews, always use the stalks as well, they give a lovely flavour.'

Gennaro Contaldo

Simon Hopkinson

Simon Hopkinson had a brilliant career as a chef, culminating in his helping to open the very successful Bibendum in London. Things have gone just as well since he turned to cookery writing: his book *Roast Chicken and Other Stories* was voted most useful cookery book of all time. This is taken from his latest wonderful book, *The Vegetarian Option*.

Macaroni cheese with tomatoes

serves 2
400ml milk
1 bay leaf
freshly grated nutmeg
salt and freshly ground white pepper
40g butter
25g plain flour
100g mature cheddar or tasty Lancashire cheese
150g macaroni
4 small ripe tomatoes, thinly sliced
1 tbs freshly grated Parmesan

To make the cheese sauce, heat the milk with the bay, nutmeg and a little salt. Simmer for a few minutes, then take off the heat, cover and allow the flavours to mingle for 10 minutes. Preheat the oven to 180°C/gas 4.

In another pan, melt the butter and stir in the flour. Cook gently for a minute or two to make a roux, but on no account allow it to colour. Remove the bay leaf, add the milk to the roux and vigorously whisk together until smooth.

Set the sauce to cook on the lowest possible heat (preferably using a heat-diffuser mat) and stir, fairly constantly, using a wooden spoon. The consistency will soon become silky and unctuous. After about 10–15 minutes, stir in the cheese, then add pepper and taste for salt. Cook for a further 3–4 minutes. Switch off the heat and cover with a tight-fitting lid; this helps prevent a skin from forming. Keep warm, nearby.

Add the macaroni to a pan of lightly salted boiling water and boil until tender, then drain very well. Mix with the cheese sauce and spoon into a lightly buttered baking dish. Cover with the tomatoes, slightly overlapping the slices, and sprinkle evenly with the Parmesan.

Bake in the oven for about 30–40 minutes, until the tomatoes are lightly blistered and the edges are bubbling up nicely, from underneath.

Mark Hix

Mark Hix, from Weymouth, first became a head chef when he was just 22. Until 2007 he was chef director at Caprice Holdings, looking after the Ivy and Le Caprice, among others. He has since opened four restaurants of his own: Hix Oyster and Chop House, HIX and HIX Selfridges in London and Hix Oyster and Fish House in Lyme Regis. This recipe first appeared in *British Seasonal Food*, one of his many acclaimed cookbooks.

Mutton and turnip hotpot

This is basically a Lancashire hotpot, incorporating turnips and potatoes. There are various versions of this traditional dish, but the main ingredient is usually a flavoursome cut of lamb, such as the neck, which is traditionally cut on the bone chops. I prefer to use mutton, as the end flavour is far better – almost gamey.

serves 4–6
1–1.5kg mutton neck chops
salt and freshly ground black pepper
plain flour for dusting
6 lambs kidneys, halved and trimmed (optional)
4–5 tbs vegetable oil
450–500g onions, peeled and thinly sliced
60g unsalted butter, plus extra, melted, for brushing
800ml lamb or beef stock
1 tsp chopped rosemary leaves
500g large potatoes
500g large turnips

Preheat the oven to 220°C/gas 7. Season the mutton chops with salt and pepper and dust with flour. Do the same with the kidneys if you're including them. Heat a heavy-based frying pan and add 2 tbs oil. Fry the chops, a few at a time, over a high heat until nicely coloured, then remove to a colander to drain. If using kidneys, fry them briefly to colour; drain and set aside.

Wipe out the pan, then add another 2 tbs oil and fry the onions over a high heat until they begin to colour. Add the butter and continue to cook for a few minutes until they soften. Dust the onions with 1 tbs flour, stir well, then gradually add the stock, stirring to avoid lumps. Sprinkle in the chopped rosemary. Bring to the boil, season with salt and pepper, then lower the heat and simmer for about 10 minutes.

Peel the potatoes and turnips and cut into 3mm slices.

To assemble, take a deep casserole dish with lid. Cover the bottom with a layer of potatoes and turnips followed by a layer of meat moistened with a little sauce, then another layer of potatoes and turnips. Continue in this way until the meat and most of the sauce have been used, ending with the turnips and finally an overlapping layer of potato slices. Brush the top with a little of the sauce.

Cover and cook in the hot oven for about 30 minutes. Now turn the oven down to 140°C/gas 1 and cook slowly for a further 2 hours or until the meat is tender.

Remove the lid and turn the oven back up to 220°C/gas 7. Brush the potato topping with a little melted butter and return to the oven for 15 minutes or so to allow the potatoes to brown.

I always keep a jar of anchovies in the cupboard, as they give a kick to all manner of dishes that would otherwise be bland, and can be used in so many ways, like adding to butter and melting over meat.

4 good things to do with leeks

Creamy cheesy leeks

This makes a nice, rich side dish to any roast: gently sweat a couple of leeks sliced into rings in butter, but don't allow to colour (discard the tough tops of the leaves). When they are soft and shiny, add a generous splash of cream (how much depends on what cream you use, and how loose you like the leeks) and a big handful of good cheddar, grated. Add more cheese or cream to thicken or loosen, or cook very gently indeed to thicken. Finish with a grind of pepper. This is a good one to prepare early and reheat quickly to serve, as it doesn't suffer from sitting in the pan with the lid on until everything else is ready (though it may need another splash of cream by then).

Leek, potato and rosemary bake

Another good side dish: sweat a couple of leeks as before, allow to lightly colour but not catch. Meanwhile, boil enough potatoes to fill your oven dish until they're just done – any boilable potato will do, but keep the skins on. Tip them into a dish and crush (don't mash) them roughly. Mix in the cooked leeks and 1 tbs finely chopped rosemary. Season and finish off with a good slug of milk all over the potatoes. Brown in a hot oven for 15 minutes or until the milk has been absorbed by the potato and the top is crispy. A generous topping of cheese before baking would transform this into a quick, cheap supper on its own.

Leeks with sausages

Get 4 good, garlicky Italian sausages and brown all over in a pan. Meanwhile, cook 2 or 3 leeks in enough stock (or water) to cover them, for about 10 minutes, until tender. Drain. Put the sausages in an ovenproof dish and cover them with the leeks, a little cream and lots of black pepper. Bake in a hot oven until bubbling, just browned on top and the sausages are cooked through.

Leeks and bacon

Make macaroni cheese (see page 41), but before browning add lardons or small pieces of bacon, fried until just crisp, and sautéed sliced leeks. Cook as normal. Or omit the macaroni and serve as a leek and bacon gratin. Or add the fried bacon to the potato bake mentioned before and omit the rosemary.

Gordon Ramsay

Gordon Ramsay is a successful celebrity chef, with Michelin-starred restaurants all over the world. His television series are tremendously popular, as are his books. This recipe first appeared in *Gordon Ramsay's World Kitchen*, a collection of his takes on recipes from around the world, inspired by the 2009 series of *The F Word*.

Rhubarb fool

Beautiful bright pink forced rhubarb makes a delicious creamy fool. The rhubarb stems break down easily when heated, so cook for less time if you prefer the fruit to hold its shape and have a firmer texture.

serves 4–6
500g rhubarb
75g soft light brown sugar
finely grated zest and juice of 1 orange
1 vanilla pod, slit open

for the custard:
150ml whole milk
250ml double cream
50g caster sugar
6 large egg yolks

Cut the rhubarb stems into short lengths and place in a saucepan with the brown sugar, orange zest and juice. Add a splash of water and scrape the seeds from the vanilla pod into the pan, using the tip of a knife. Place over a high heat. When the liquid begins to bubble, lower the heat and simmer gently for 8–10 minutes or until the rhubarb is tender. Remove from the heat and allow to cool completely, then chill.

Now make the custard. Put the milk, cream and 1 tbs sugar into a heavy-based saucepan and slowly bring to the boil. Meanwhile, beat the eggs and the rest of the sugar together in a large bowl, using a hand whisk, until light and creamy. Just before the creamy milk comes to the boil, gradually pour it onto the egg and sugar mixture, whisking continuously. Strain the mixture through a fine sieve back into the pan and place over a low heat. Stir constantly with a wooden spoon until the custard thickens enough to coat the back of the spoon; do not overheat or it will curdle. Remove from the heat and strain through a fine sieve once more. Pour into a chilled bowl and allow to cool, stirring every so often to prevent a skin from forming. Chill until needed.

When ready to serve, lightly fold two-thirds of the chilled rhubarb through the chilled custard. Drop a small spoonful of rhubarb into each serving glass, then top with the rippled fool. Spoon the remaining rhubarb on top and serve straight away.

March

Purple sprouting broccoli, cauliflowers, leeks, parsley, radishes, early rhubarb, spring greens, spring onions and wild garlic are all good this month.

This month, experiment with
Anjum Anand's delicious scrambled tofu and as the weather gets slightly warmer, tuck into Mark Hix's scallops or Gordon Ramsay's mussels. Treat yourself with a quick and easy cake – either Eric Chavot's delicious Twix and banana cake, or Giorgio Locatelli's egg-free chocolate cake.

Gordon Ramsay

Moules marinières

Rope-grown mussels are now widely available pretty much all year round, which means we can enjoy this lovely dish any time. It is equally suited to warm and chill days. Serve in deep soup bowls with home-made chips if you like, plus mayonnaise and lots of crusty bread to mop up the flavourful juice.

serves 4

1kg live mussels
1 onion, peeled and finely chopped
1 shallot, peeled and finely chopped
1 clove of garlic, finely chopped
1 bay leaf
3 sprigs of thyme
a handful of flat-leaf parsley, stalks separated, leaves chopped
200ml dry white wine
black pepper

Scrub the mussels clean under cold running water, scraping off any barnacles with a knife and tugging away any beards. Check over the mussels, discarding any that are cracked or open and do not close when sharply tapped. Rinse well and set aside.

Place the onion, shallot, garlic, bay leaf, thyme, parsley stalks and wine in a large pan. Bring to the boil, then tip in the mussels and cover the pan with a tight-fitting lid. Give the pan one or two shakes, then let the mussels steam for 3–4 minutes until they have opened. Discard any that remain closed. Season with a good grinding of pepper. Mussels are naturally salty, so you probably won't need to add salt.

Divide the mussels and cooking juices between warm large bowls and sprinkle with the chopped parsley. Serve immediately, remembering to provide bowls for the discarded empty shells.

(This recipe is from *Gordon Ramsay's World Kitchen*.)

I always keep some tins of Napolina tomatoes in the cupboard for making quick tomato and basil soup, a spicy salsa or some penne arrabbiata.

Gennaro Contaldo

Gennaro Contaldo was born in Minori on the Amalfi Coast. He has an award-winning Italian restaurant in London called Passione and he regularly appears on British and American television. He is well known for acting as a mentor to Jamie Oliver, and was involved with the setting up of the chain Jamie's Kitchen. This is actually Jamie Oliver's favourite recipe. His latest book is called *Gennaro's Easy Italian*, and he has also just started giving outdoor cookery classes.

Pasta alla puttanesca

serves 4

4 tbs Evo (Jordanian extra-virgin olive oil – or you can use ordinary extra-virgin)
2 cloves of garlic, left whole and crushed with the flat blade of a knife
½ small red chilli, finely chopped (optional)
3 anchovy fillets
20 black olives, stoned and sliced in half or left whole
1 tbs capers
140g tin of plum tomatoes, chopped
½ tsp dried oregano
a handful of parsley, finely chopped
350g linguine or spaghetti
salt to taste

Heat the oil in a large frying pan, and add the garlic, chilli and anchovy fillets. Fry until the garlic is golden brown, then discard with the chilli if you prefer. Fry the anchovies until they have melted. Add the olives and capers and stir-fry for a minute. Then add the tomatoes, oregano and parsley. Lower the heat, cover with a lid and simmer gently for 20 minutes. In the meantime, cook the pasta until al dente. When cooked, drain and add to the sauce. Stir well and continue to cook for a further minute, so that the pasta absorbs all the flavours. If you find it is too dry, add a couple of tbs of the hot pasta water. Serve immediately.

I love good Italian extra-virgin olive oil and Amalfi lemons. With these two ingredients I can both dress salads and cook, and the lemons remind me of home.

John Torode

John Torode is an Australian chef and restaurateur. He came to the UK aged 25 and worked in several well-known restaurants before starting his own, Smiths of Smithfield, and in 2009, The LUXE Spitalfields. He often appears on TV, and is especially well known for his role as a judge on the successful MasterChef series. He has written several very popular books, including *John Torode's Beef and Other Bovine Matters* and *John Torode's Chicken and Other Birds*.

Sunday roast

Simple roast beef

Get a good quality, big, four-bone rib of beef, score the fat and salt it. Put it in the oven at 180°C/gas 4 for 2 1/2 hours, take it out and let it rest, covered, for half an hour. Delicious every time. Serves 8 very generously.

Great potatoes

Get the fat for the potatoes hot before they go in the oven, and turn them in it thoroughly, then you won't need to keep basting them. Don't keep opening the oven door. Put the meat in. Keep the door shut until you put in your potatoes (an hour before you serve the meat). When you have taken the meat out, turn the oven up to 210°C/gas 6 1/2 to finish off the potatoes and don't open the door again until you put in the Yorkshires (about 10 minutes before you serve the meat).

Perfect Yorkshires

While the meat is resting, use its fat for your Yorkshires. Pop a splash of fat into each of the moulds in a muffin tray and get it hot in the oven. You can use powdered mix, it works just as well, or you can make your own batter, but make it the night before. Make double the quantity, keep half back, clean the tray and put a little butter in each mould. After the main course, make another round, but this time, serve them sprinkled with icing sugar and some damson jam and ice cream.

Quick and easy gravy

Scrape the bottom of your roasting tin, getting up all the stuck-on meat and pan juices. Put it on the heat and add half a handful of flour and some water. Then stir and stir and stir. At first the flour will go lumpy and look like wet breadcrumbs, but as you keep stirring it will turn into perfect gravy. Do not add red wine. Firstly, wine is for drinking. Secondly, wine stops the flour working properly.

Vivek Singh

Home-style curry of potatoes and cauliflower (Aloo gobhi)

This is probably the most common and basic vegetable curry you will find anywhere in India. Cooked pretty much nine months of the year, it is one of those recipes that spark an intense debate over authenticity. One of the disadvantages of its universal appeal is that there is no such thing as a universal recipe!

serves 4

3 tbs vegetable or corn oil
1 tsp cumin seeds
1 large onion, chopped
1 tbs ginger-garlic paste (crushed garlic and ginger mixed together)
4 green chillies, slit open lengthwise
2 medium potatoes, peeled and cut into 2.5cm dice

1 cauliflower, divided into florets
1 tsp ground turmeric
2 tsp salt
2 tomatoes, chopped
½ tsp garam masala
1 tbs chopped fresh coriander
5cm piece of fresh ginger, cut into fine strips
juice of ½ a lime

Heat the oil in a wide, shallow pan and add the cumin seeds, followed by the onion. Sauté for about 5 minutes, until the onion is soft, then add the ginger-garlic paste and fry for a few seconds longer. Add the green chillies and potatoes and sauté over a high heat for a couple of minutes. Tip in the cauliflower, turmeric and salt, mix well, then reduce the heat. Cover the pan and cook for about 10 minutes, stirring occasionally to prevent sticking.

Add the tomatoes and garam masala and cook for about 5 minutes, until the vegetables are completely tender. Sprinkle in the chopped coriander and the ginger, squeeze over the lime juice and serve – either with chapattis or as a side dish.

Tips: If you cut the cauliflower florets slightly bigger than the potatoes, they will cook in roughly the same time, rather than overcooking and disintegrating before the potatoes are done. It's important to use a wide, shallow pan for this dish. If you use a deep pan or a wok instead, don't overcrowd it with the vegetables or they will start to disintegrate.

(This recipe is from *Curry: Classic and Contemporary*.)

Black onion seeds (Nigella seeds): I love these as a spice, they're dramatic and beautifully nutty with breads and with seafood. I love the surprise element that they bring to most dishes.

Anjum Anand

Anjum Anand has worked in restaurants such as Café Spice in New York, the Mondrian in Los Angeles and the Park Royal Hotel's Indian restaurant in New Delhi. She regularly appears on TV around the world championing her lighter version of Indian food. She has written four books, the latest of which is *Anjum's Eat Right for Your Body Type*, which is about cooking inspired by the principles of Ayurveda and where this recipe first appeared.

Spicy scrambled tofu
This dish is a great breakfast or brunch dish as it is warming and nourishing but light. I eat this with a little plain wholemeal toast or as part of a meal with flatbreads.

serves 1
1 tsp ghee or vegetable oil
1 green chilli, pierced with the tip of a knife
½ a small onion, peeled and finely chopped (around 3 tbs)
½ a small clove of garlic, peeled and finely chopped
½ a medium tomato, chopped
½ tsp garam masala
½ tsp ground cumin
⅛ tsp ground turmeric
salt and freshly milled black pepper
100g firm tofu, chopped into small pieces
a small handful of fresh coriander leaves, chopped

Heat the ghee or oil in a small non-stick frying pan. Add the chilli and onion and sauté until golden at the edges. Add the garlic and cook for 30–40 seconds. Add the tomato, spices and seasoning and cook over a medium heat for 3–4 minutes or until the tomatoes have softened.

Add the tofu and a splash of warm water, then cook for 5 minutes, breaking up and squashing the pieces so the tofu resembles scrambled eggs (I use the back of my wooden spoon, but a potato masher would probably be quicker). Sprinkle over the coriander and serve hot.

TRICKS OF THE TRADE

'You can keep rice for up to 12 years, and the older it is, the better it gets. I like to buy rice and forget about it in the cupboard for a couple of years – it's delicious!'

Vivek Singh

4 good things to do with eggs

Posh baked eggs with spinach and mushrooms

Roast an upturned, whole portobello mushroom per person in the oven with a knob of butter and some roughly chopped garlic inside the cup. Wilt a big handful of spinach per person and once cooked put a layer into a well-buttered ramekin each. Crack a whole egg over the spinach, being careful not to break the yolk. Season and bake in a medium oven until the white is just set – about 10 mins. Serve in the ramekins with the mushrooms, a slice of garlic sourdough (see page 177) or toast and perhaps a scattering of Parmesan.

Posh baked eggs with smoked haddock

Poach a small piece of smoked haddock briefly in milk and leave to cool. Drain and crumble it into the bottom of a couple of buttered ramekins. Break an egg over the top of each, carefully as before. Season and bake in a medium oven till the white is set. Serve with lots of snipped chives and a little dressed green salad.

Spanish-style omelette with feta

Fry a couple of sliced onions and a parboiled, diced potato in a little olive oil in an ovenproof frying pan. Add some strips of red pepper and cook until soft and the onion and potato are just golden. Crumble in a handful of feta, half a tsp of chopped rosemary and some black pepper, mix briefly and then pour in 4 eggs, beaten and mixed with a little milk. Allow to cook, without stirring, for 3–4 minutes, until the edges begin to set and the bottom begins to brown. Put the lid on and cook a little longer until the egg is set – you can stick it under a very hot grill briefly to brown the top. Serve in slices; the middle should be slightly wobbly.

One-pot eggs and chorizo

Chop 3 cooking chorizo sausages per person into chunks, and slice an onion. Fry in a frying pan until the sausage is browned and the onions are soft. Make 3 or 4 wells in the mixture and break a whole egg into each one. Put the lid on and cook on a medium heat for a couple of minutes, until the egg is just set and the yolk still runny. Take off the heat as soon as they are ready as they will carry on cooking in the pan. Shower the eggs with chopped coriander and eat straight from the pan with crusty bread to dip in the yolks. Make this even heartier by adding cubes of parboiled potato at the beginning, and/or a couple of chopped tomatoes.

Mark Hix

Scallops with purple-sprouting broccoli

Sprouting broccoli isn't often paired with such posh partners, but it is a perfect foil for firm sweet scallops and makes a great seasonal starter. Ideally, buy scallops in the shell and prepare them yourself, or at least buy them freshly shucked. I now keep the muscle on scallops, as it seems such a waste to trim it off. Likewise, I don't discard the corals. Here I've sautéed them until they start to crisp up to give them an appetising texture.

serves 4
8 small tender stems of purple-sprouting broccoli
salt and freshly ground black pepper
100g butter
12 medium scallops, shelled and cleaned

Trim the nice purple heads and a few leaves from the sprouting broccoli and put to one side. Chop the rest and cook in a pan of boiling salted water for 4–5 minutes until tender, then drain and whizz in a blender or food processor until smooth. Transfer to a clean pan, season with salt and pepper to taste and add a couple of knobs of the butter; keep warm.

Remove the corals from the scallops and cut in half if large. Heat about a third of the remaining butter in a heavy-based frying pan. Season the corals and fry for 4–5 minutes, turning them every so often until crisp.

Meanwhile, add the purple heads and leaves to a pan of boiling salted water and cook for about 3 minutes until tender, then drain.

When the corals are crisp, remove and set aside. Wipe out the pan, then rub some of the remaining butter over the base and place over a medium-high heat. Season the scallops and cook for just 1 minute each side, then add the rest of the butter, the fried corals and the broccoli heads and leaves.

Spoon the broccoli purée onto warm plates, arrange the scallops, corals and broccoli on top and serve at once.

(This recipe is from *British Seasonal Food*.)

Shane Osborn

Ragout of borlotti beans and baby onions

serves 6

175g borlotti beans or dried haricot blanc beans (soaked in cold water for 24 hours)
1 carrot, peeled and cut into quarters
1 stick of celery, peeled and cut into quarters
1 onion, peeled and cut into quarters
3 cloves of garlic, peeled
5–6 sprigs of fresh thyme
100g smoked bacon, kept in large pieces
2l chicken stock
20 baby onions, peeled and the bottoms just trimmed of the roots
75g unsalted butter, chilled and cubed
5–6 sprigs of tarragon leaves, picked and finely chopped
½ a lemon
salt and black pepper

Strain the pre-soaked beans and put in a large saucepan. Cover with fresh water and bring to the boil. Once boiling, strain off the water, return the beans to the same pan and add the carrot, celery, onion, garlic, thyme and bacon. Cover with about 2 litres of stock, bring the beans to a gentle boil and allow to cook until tender, stirring occasionally, for about 45 minutes. Remove from the heat and allow the beans to cool in their liquor.

When the beans are sufficiently cool, strain, reserving the liquor in a large saucepan. Return the liquor to the heat, add the peeled baby onions and simmer for 10–12 minutes until tender. Set aside the onions, bring the liquor back to boil and reduce it by half. Remove all the bacon and vegetables from the cool beans and discard.

Whisk the cold butter into the reduced cooking liquor to emulsify the sauce, add the beans and baby onions, simmer for a few moments to warm through and add the chopped tarragon. The consistency should be thick and soupy. Check the seasoning, adding a squeeze of lemon if you like, and serve.

Paul Rankin

Paul Rankin's first restaurant, Roscoff, in Belfast, opened in 1989 and won the region's first Michelin star. Before this, he and his wife Jeanne had worked for and trained under Albert Roux. They now have a second restaurant, Cayenne. Paul often appears on television, has written five books and has his own food brand.

Piri-piri hake with prawns and chickpea salad

serves 4
2 tbs piri piri paste
4 x 150g fillets of hake
1 x 300g prawns, raw, peeled and digestive tract removed
salt and pepper
1 tbs light olive oil

for the chickpeas:
300g chickpeas, soaked overnight
1 carrot
1 medium onion
4 cloves of garlic

for the hummus:
1 tsp tahini
1 tsp chopped garlic
2 tbs lemon juice
50–100ml olive oil

for the chickpea salad:
1 tsp lemon zest
¼ tsp chopped garlic
1 tbs chopped parsley
1 tbs lemon juice
50ml extra-virgin olive oil

rocket or pea shoots to garnish

First cook the chickpeas: cover them in water, adding the carrot, onion and the garlic. Simmer for 1–2 hours until tender. Drain, reserving the liquor. Add a little salt and divide, leaving a quarter to one side.

Blend the remaining three quarters of the chickpeas with tahini, garlic, lemon juice and olive oil to make a hummus. You'll need a generous tbs per person, loosened with a bit of the cooking liquor. You could keep the rest in the fridge for when you have the munchies.

Smear the hake fillets and toss the prawns in the piri-piri paste. Season lightly with salt and pepper and put a non-stick frying pan with light olive oil over a high heat. Cook the hake skin-side down for 3–4 minutes until nicely crisp, then turn it over and add the prawns, cook for a minute, then let it all rest in the pan, off the heat.

Mix the reserved whole chickpeas with the lemon zest, garlic, parsley, lemon juice, 1 tbs chickpea cooking liquor, salt, pepper and extra-virgin olive oil. Warm in a microwave for 30 seconds and do the same with the hummus.

Carefully spoon some of the diluted hummus onto 4 warm plates. Add the hake then surround with the prawns and the chickpeas, and garnish with some wild rocket or pea shoots.

4 good things to do with cauliflower

Spicy fried cauliflower

Serve this as a side to curry or with meat or fish. Blanch a head of cauliflower, broken into small florets, in boiling water for a minute. Drain and dry on kitchen paper. Toast some whole spices (cumin seeds, coriander seeds and/or black mustard seeds) in a hot pan until they crackle, then bash them up briefly with a pestle and mortar and add a pinch of salt. Fry the cauliflower pieces in a little vegetable oil until golden, and then at the last minute sprinkle over the spices and cook for 30 seconds.

Cauliflower salad with anchovies

Cook cauliflower florets until tender, then drain and allow to cool. Make a dressing with a couple of chopped anchovies, a little mustard, finely chopped capers, parsley and good olive oil. Toss the cooled cauliflower in the dressing.

Stir-fried cauliflower with chilli

Break up raw cauliflower into small florets and stir-fry quickly in very hot vegetable oil with a crushed clove of garlic and some slices of red chilli. Season with a little salt to serve. Eat while hot and crunchy.

Roasted cauliflower

Add a broken-up cauliflower to your usual roasting veg – it will need to cook for about 25–35 minutes in a little olive oil, and you should turn it occasionally. This will work just as well mixed with more Mediterranean-style roasted veg, like aubergine, red onion and peppers, as it will with winter vegetables like parsnips.

Bill Granger

Bill Granger was born in Australia, where he has three restaurants, plus another in Tokyo. He is a self-taught chef and food writer and his television programmes are broadcast in 27 countries. His latest book showcasing his laidback, straightforward cookery, which contains this recipe, is called *Feed Me Now*.

Lemon posset

serves 8
180ml lemon juice – about 4 lemons
125g caster sugar
500ml double cream
slivered unsalted pistachio nuts or berries to serve

Strain the lemon juice into a medium saucepan, add the sugar and stir over a low heat until the sugar has dissolved. Take off the heat.

Meanwhile, pour the cream into another small saucepan and bring to the boil. Whisk the cream into the sweetened lemon juice until combined. Pour into 8 shot glasses and chill until set, about 3 hours.

Serve sprinkled with a few pistachio nuts, or some berries.

Eric Chavot

Eric Chavot is a Michelin-starred chef who grew up near Bordeaux. He has worked for Marco Pierre White and for Pierre Koffman at La Tante Claire and his recent pop-up restaurant. He spent 10 years as head chef of the Capital Hotel in London, where he won two Michelin stars.

Twix and banana cake

In France we have a cake which is similar to your pound cake, called the 'quatre quart' cake, made with the same amount of all four ingredients. So if you have three eggs, weigh them and then use the same weights of butter, sugar and flour.

makes 1 cake
3 eggs, weighed and separated, whites beaten until stiff
an equal quantity of butter
the same of sugar
the same of flour
an over-ripe banana
1 Twix bar

Cream the butter and sugar, add the eggs and sifted flour. Then take an old banana and lightly caramelise it in a hot pan. Break it up and add to the mixture. Finally crumble a Twix and mix in. Cook the cake in a sponge tin for about 45 mins at 180°C / gas 4 until a skewer inserted into the middle comes out clean. The finished cake will have lovely biscuity, toffee and chocolate chunks in it.

Giorgio Locatelli

Margherita's eggless chocolate cake

serves 8
450g plain flour (organic if possible)
6 tbs unsweetened cocoa powder (e.g. Green & Black's)
2 tsp baking powder
2 tsp bicarbonate of soda
300g caster sugar
125ml vegetable oil
300ml water
2 tbs distilled white vinegar
2 tsp vanilla extract

for the icing:
'It's all mine' dark chocolate spread, by English Provender Company, or similar
or:
225g icing sugar
25g unsweetened cocoa powder
75g butter, diced
1 tbs golden syrup
4 tbs milk
whipped cream to decorate

Preheat the oven to 180°C/gas 4. Sift the flour, cocoa powder, baking powder and bicarbonate of soda into a large bowl and stir in the sugar. Combine all the wet ingredients in another bowl. Pour the wet ingredients into the dry ingredients and beat until smooth. Pour the batter into a greased 23cm/9in springform cake tin and bake for about an hour, until a skewer inserted in the centre comes out clean (place a sheet of foil over the top of the cake if it becomes too dark). Remove from the oven and leave to cool in the tin.

Turn the cake out of the tin and spread the chocolate spread over the top. Or, if you are making your own icing, sift the icing sugar and cocoa powder into a bowl and make a well in the centre. Gently heat the butter, golden syrup and milk until the butter has melted, then pour into the well in the dry ingredients and stir until smooth. Beat with a wooden spoon until the icing has cooled and thickened slightly. Spread the icing over the top and sides of the cake with a palette knife. Decorate with whipped cream.

April

New season's lettuce and watercress, radishes and purple sprouting broccoli are all good this month, along with Jersey Royals, spring greens, morels, outdoor rhubarb and wood pigeon (which is available most of the year, but fattest in spring).

This month, make the most of the new potatoes arriving, with Martin Nisbet's twist on a potato salad with smoked haddock, Paul Merret's wood pigeon with Jersey Royals or Simon Rimmer's vegetarian coronation chickpeas. Finish off with Skye Gyngell's dangerously good warm chocolate puddings.

Bill Granger

Baked whole fish with lemon potatoes

Whole fish can seem daunting to novice cooks, but here it is easy to handle. With the protective herb-paste coating you can just pop the whole thing in the oven.

serves 4
2 x 800g white fish, such as small bass, cleaned and scaled
a handful of coriander leaves
10 spring onions, chopped
1 tsp chilli flakes
2 tbs extra-virgin olive oil
1 tsp salt

for the lemon potatoes:
1kg yellow waxy potatoes
3 tbs extra-virgin olive oil
3 cloves of garlic, crushed
sea salt and freshly ground black pepper
125ml fish or chicken stock
60ml lemon juice
100g pitted black olives, roughly chopped
a small handful flat-leaf parsley, finely chopped

Preheat the oven to 200°C/gas 6. For the lemon potatoes, cut the potatoes into thick slices and place in a roasting tray. Add the olive oil, garlic, salt, pepper, stock and lemon juice and toss with your hands to combine. Bake in the oven for 25 minutes, stirring every 10 minutes.

Meanwhile, make 3 slashes on each side of the fish through the thickest part and place on a baking tray. Put the remaining ingredients into a food processor and process to a coarse paste. Spread the paste over each side of the fish and into the slashes.

Lower the oven setting to 180°C/gas 4 and put the fish into the oven (below the potatoes). Bake for 20 minutes or until it is cooked through, adding the olives and parsley to the potatoes for the last 5 minutes. Serve at once, placing the fish on top of the potatoes if you like.

(This recipe is from *Feed Me Now*.)

Tim Hughes

The Ivy's salmon fishcakes with sorrel sauce
This was originally on the menu at Le Caprice and was brought over to The Ivy's menu, where it is a favourite.

serves 4
325g potato, mashed (without milk or butter)
325g salmon fillet, poached in salted water for 3–4 minutes
1 tbs tomato ketchup
1 tbs anchovy essence
1 tbs English mustard
salt and pepper

for the sauce:
250–300ml strong fish stock (a cube will do)
25g butter
1 tbs flour
25ml white wine
100ml double cream
fresh sorrel leaves (about 5), shredded
700–800g spinach, picked over, washed and dried

To make the fishcakes, mix together the potato, half the poached salmon, the ketchup, anchovy essence, mustard and seasoning until it is smooth. Flake the remaining salmon and fold it in gently. Mould the mixture into 8 round cakes and refrigerate.

To make the sauce, bring the fish stock to the boil in a thick-bottomed pan. In another pan melt the butter and stir in the flour. Cook very slowly over a low heat for 30 seconds, then whisk the fish stock into the flour mixture. Pour in the wine and simmer for 30 minutes until the sauce has thickened. Add the cream and reduce the sauce until it is of a thick pouring consistency, then stir in the sorrel and season.

Lightly flour the fishcakes and fry in vegetable oil until coloured on both sides, or brush them with oil and cook for 10–15 minutes in a moderately hot oven (200°C/gas 6).

Remove the stalks from the spinach, wash and shake off as much water as possible. Heat a large pan over a medium flame, add the spinach, lightly season with salt and pepper and cover tightly with a lid. Cook for 3–4 minutes, stirring occasionally, until the leaves are tender. Drain in a colander to remove excess water.

Divide the spinach between 4 warmed plates, place 2 of the fishcakes on top and pour over the sauce. Serve immediately.

Andy MacKenzie

Andy MacKenzie is the executive chef at the Avenue restaurant at Lainston House Hotel in Hampshire. He started working there in 1986 and worked his way up to head chef in 2001. He has twice won Hampshire's chef of the year.

Trout and watercress terrine

serves 8 as a starter
200g (approx.) long sliced smoked salmon
800g fresh trout, pin-boned and skinned
salt and pepper
lemon zest
300g butter
2 bunches of watercress (stalks removed)

Lay out three sheets of cling film one on top of the other on a work surface, ensuring there is no air between them. Use these to line a small terrine mould or a loaf tin. Layer the smoked salmon to line the mould; the slices should overlap each other and there should be excess hanging from the sides.

Meanwhile, place the trout on a baking tray and season with salt and pepper and the lemon zest. Melt the butter and pour over the fish, then bake it in the oven at 200°C/ gas 6 for 7 minutes – the fish should just be cooked.

Place two fillets of the fish in the bottom of the mould and press with your hands to pack it into the bottom. Now add a layer of the watercress (the heat from the fish will wilt it). Repeat this process until the mould is full and the layers reach slightly above the sides of the mould.

Pour any remaining juice from the baking tray into the terrine. Fold the salmon back over the trout so that it is all covered – use more if necessary. Pull the remaining cling film tight and wrap the fish in it, over the top. Pierce small holes in it with a knife. Place another terrine mould, or something similar, on the top and press down. Place weights on top and refrigerate for at least 4 hours. To serve, cut the terrine into slices.

4 good things to do with lettuce

Lettuce with peas
Cut a romaine or little gem lettuce into strips. Heat a little butter gently in a pan and add the lettuce, allow it to wilt just slightly and stir in some warm, cooked peas. You could also add some chopped chives. Stir together, taste and adjust the seasoning, and serve as a side dish.

Lettuce instead of a burger bun
Cook yourself a nice burger – meat, fish, veggie, it doesn't matter. Slather it in your favourite condiments. Take a big leaf from a round lettuce and sit the burger on it. Stack with pickles, tomato or cucumber, cheese even. Then wrap the lettuce leaf around the burger and eat it. (This is inspired by a Nigel Slater recipe.)

Lettuce soup
Gently cook a couple of chopped spring onions in butter, then add a roughly shredded head of lettuce and allow to wilt. (You could also add peas here.) Add a few mint leaves, and perhaps some parsley. Cover with hot stock (chicken or vegetable), simmer briefly and season. Blend and serve. You could add a splash of cream to thicken it, if you like.

Stir-fried lettuce
Crispy lettuces are good for this – iceberg works well. Stir-fry wide strips of lettuce in sesame oil and a little soy sauce. Sprinkle with toasted sesame seeds if you have some handy.

TRICKS OF THE TRADE

*'Even when you think your sauce is ready, always add
a pinch of seasoning or a touch of acidity.'*

Jérôme Ponchelle

Yotam Ottolenghi and Sami Tamimi

Yotam Ottolenghi did a master's in philosophy and literature before becoming a chef. He worked at Launceston Place, Maison Blanc and Baker and Spice before starting his own restaurant-and-food-shops, Ottolenghi, which he runs with Sami Tamimi. Their first book, *Ottolenghi: the Cookbook*, was a word-of-mouth bestseller and where this recipe was first published. Their latest book is called *Plenty*.

Roast chicken with saffron, hazelnuts and honey

This dish is inspired by a recipe from Claudia Roden's classic book, Tamarind and Saffron. It is one of our favourites: it is so easy to make, yet looks stunning, and has the most delicate and exotic combination of flavours (rosewater, saffron and cinnamon), which takes you straight to the famous Jamaa el Fna in Marrakech. Serve with rice or plain couscous.

serves 4

1 large organic or free-range chicken, divided into quarters: breast + wing and leg + thigh
2 onions, roughly chopped
4 tbs olive oil
1 tsp ground ginger
1 tsp ground cinnamon
a generous pinch of saffron strands
juice of 1 lemon
4 tbs cold water
2 tsp coarse sea salt
1 tsp black pepper
100g unskinned hazelnuts
70g honey
2 tbs rosewater
2 spring onions, roughly chopped

In a large bowl, mix the chicken pieces with the onions, olive oil, ginger, cinnamon, saffron, lemon juice, water, salt and pepper. Leave to marinate for at least an hour, or overnight in the fridge.

Preheat the oven to 190°C/gas 5. Spread the hazelnuts out on an oven tray and roast for 10 minutes, until lightly browned. Chop roughly and set aside.

Transfer the chicken and marinade to a roasting tray large enough to accommodate everything comfortably. Arrange the chicken pieces skin-side up and put the tray in the oven for about 35 minutes.

While the chicken is roasting, mix the honey, rosewater and nuts together to make a rough paste. Remove the chicken from the oven, spoon a generous amount of nut paste onto each piece and spread it to cover. Return to the oven for 5–10 minutes, until the chicken is cooked through and the nuts are golden brown. Transfer the chicken to a serving dish and garnish with the chopped spring onions.

Paul Merrett

Paul Merrett is the chef and joint proprietor of the Victoria in East Sheen, London, and regularly appears on television in the UK. Before the Victoria he worked at the Ritz and the Greenhouse in Mayfair. He recently published his first book, the story of his mission to feed his own family by living off an allotment, called *Using the Plot*. He also co-presented *Economy Gastronomy* with Allegra McEvedy.

Warm wood pigeon salad

Wood pigeon is very cheap and yet extremely tasty. Wild garlic, fried potatoes and bacon give the salad a real richness, which is balanced by the vinaigrette. Morel mushrooms are a complete luxury but entirely worth it.

serves 4

2 sticks of rhubarb
1 dsp caster sugar
a little cider vinegar
200ml very light olive oil
2 plump wood pigeon

a handful of salad leaves per person
100g streaky bacon cut into lardons
handful of fresh morel mushrooms
8 new potatoes boiled in their skins
about 16 wild garlic leaves chopped
3cm wide

Chop up the rhubarb into 3cm chunks and place in a pan. Sprinkle with 1 dsp caster sugar. Place the pan of rhubarb and sugar on the stove and allow to simmer very gently. When the rhubarb is cooked through, purée it using a jug or stick blender. Cool the purée, then add the cider vinegar to the rhubarb and whisk in the oil. The vinaigrette should be as thick as single cream and a good blend of sharp and sweet. Take care not to lose the fruitiness of the vinaigrette with too much vinegar – add it bit by bit.

About half an hour before serving the salad, cook the pigeons. Lightly rub each with a little oil and sear all over in a hot pan until brown. Transfer the pigeons to the oven – 175°C/gas 4 for about 10–15 minutes depending on size. Remove the pigeons from the oven and rest in a warm place for 10 minutes. Remove the breasts (the legs and carcass would make a great base for a game broth).

Prepare the leaves and place in a large bowl – lightly dress them with just a little of the vinaigrette. Heat a non-stick frying pan and fry the bacon pieces until caramelised, then set aside. Cook the morels in the same way and set aside too.

Break the potatoes into large chunks and fry in the pan until lightly crispy – return the bacon and mushrooms to the pan. Chuck in the wild garlic and quickly toss everything together – take off the heat and add to the leaves.

Mix the salad carefully and divide between 4 large serving bowls. Slice each pigeon breast in half and lay on top of the salad. Put a few drops of vinaigrette around the plate.

Henry Dimbleby
A simple ceviche

Slice any very fresh white fish as finely as possible (I like bass), and finely slice some firm radishes and shallots. Season and soak in lemon or lime juice for 30 minutes. Drain and lay on a plate with thin slices of ripe avocado, drizzled with olive oil and sprinkled with finely chopped coriander. Eat with sourdough bread and very cold white wine.

Michel Roux Jr
Spicy crab with avocado

Buy the best-quality fresh-picked claw meat you can find. Put the white crab meat into a bowl and add 1 avocado, 2 thinly sliced spring onions, the juice of a couple of limes, sesame oil, salt and Tabasco. Mix gently with a fork. Place a spoonful of brown meat in each serving dish, then add the white meat mixture. Garnish with watercress.

Henry Harris
Mimolette, red onion and watercress salad

Make a salad of watercress and finely sliced red onion. Use a vegetable peeler to shave a generous pile of Mimolette cheese over the top.

Sam and Eddie Hart
Baby gem lettuce, anchovy and pancetta

Cut lettuces lengthways into four wedges and drape 1 or 2 anchovies on each wedge. For the dressing, mix extra-virgin olive oil and lemon juice with a little finely diced shallot, chopped flat-leaf parsley and season with salt and pepper. Fry thin strips of pancetta until crisp. To assemble, drizzle dressing over the baby gem and add the pancetta.

Martin Nisbet

Martin Nisbet is head chef of critically acclaimed restaurant Angelus in London. He was born in Edinburgh and grew up in Scotland but came to London to work at the Savoy, which he did for six years. After two years as head chef at Anton's in Herefordshire, he returned to London to head up Angelus.

Warm salad of Jersey Royals, smoked haddock and curry oil

serves 4

50g medium curry powder
100ml groundnut oil
350g Jersey Royal new potatoes
300g naturally smoked haddock
200ml milk
a bunch of finely chopped spring onions
½ a bunch of finely chopped chives
50g mayonnaise
50g crème fraiche
salt and pepper
50g mixed salad leaves

To make the curry oil, place most of the curry powder in a pan (reserving 1 tsp) with a little groundnut oil and cook gently for 2–3 minutes. Add the remaining groundnut oil and warm gently for 5 minutes. Remove from the heat and allow to infuse for a further 30 minutes. Once infused, drain the oil through a coffee filter and keep till needed.

Scrub the Jersey Royals under cold water to remove any dirt. Steam the potatoes over boiling water till cooked. Once the potatoes are cooked, remove from the steamer and allow to cool slightly. Cut the potatoes into ½ cm slices and cover with cling film to keep them warm.

Meanwhile, cover the smoked haddock with milk and simmer gently for 5 minutes, then remove from the heat. Remove the haddock from the milk, peel off any skin and flake the fish, removing any bones.

Mix the warm fish with the potatoes. Add the spring onions and chives, then add the mayonnaise and crème fraiche and season to taste with salt, pepper and the remaining curry powder. Place the potato salad in the middle of a plate, dress the leaves with a little curry oil and place on top of the salad, and drizzle the remaining curry oil around the plate. Serve straight away.

My SECRET ingredient

Caraway seeds are used a lot in mainland Europe, but less so here. They are a great addition to roasted or braised pork. Use in the sauce or roll the meat in some seeds before cooking for a flavoursome finish.

Simon Rimmer

Simon Rimmer bought an established vegetarian café in Manchester in 1992 and although a meat-eater, decided to keep it veggie. The restaurant, Greens, is still a roaring success today. He is resident chef on BBC2's *Something for the Weekend* and has written several books, the third of which is called *The Accidental Vegetarian*.

Coronation chickpeas and Jersey potato salad

I used to think coronation chicken was really naff; it probably still is, but I love it. Well, it set me thinking: why wasn't anything created for veggies? So, by Royal Appointment, here is something for them.

serves 4 with other dishes

800g Jersey spuds, scrubbed
a bunch of spring onions, finely chopped
2 tbs vinaigrette
salt and freshly ground black pepper
300ml mayonnaise
50g smooth curry paste, maybe softened in a little hot water (any jar of curry paste will do)
100g tinned chickpeas, drained and rinsed
1 tbs sultanas
1 tbs flaked, toasted almonds
fresh coriander leaves, to garnish

Cook the spuds and, while they are still hot, cut into quarters and put in a bowl with the onions and vinaigrette. Toss them well (the spuds will absorb the dressing) and season with salt and pepper. Leave to cool.

Mix the mayo with the curry paste, then stir into the cooled spuds with the chickpeas, sultanas and almonds. Garnish with coriander leaves.

Add rosewater to any dessert for a lovely perfume (really good with strawberries and other soft fruits). It's also good in curry.

4 good things to do with mozzarella

Mozzarella and pasta

Get a packet of the harder (cheaper) cooking mozzarella. Cut a 6cm chunk of it into 2cm cubes. Thinly slice an onion and gently fry in olive oil until soft. Tip in a tin of chopped tinned tomatoes (or some chopped fresh ones) and a crushed clove of garlic. Let bubble for a few minutes. Meanwhile, cook some pasta. When the pasta is ready, taste the sauce (it shouldn't taste of raw tomatoes, but it will still taste lighter and sharper than a slow-cooked tomato sauce), season and stir in the cubed cheese and a few torn-up basil leaves. Quickly stir the whole lot into the pasta and serve before the cheese melts completely. A slightly studenty supper.

Mozzarella and tomatoes

Get some really good mozzarella. Splash it with a little good olive oil and put on a plate with some sliced, salted tomatoes. Eat.

Mozzarella quesadillas

Get 2 flour tortillas and cover one in a mixture of cooked chicken (optional, or you could use ham), strips of lightly cooked pepper, coriander leaves and sliced red onion. Rip a ball of buffalo mozzarella into shreds and scatter over the tortilla. Season. Put the other tortilla on top. Cook for 2–3 minutes each side in a hot frying pan with a little oil until the tortilla is golden and the cheese molten and oozing. Cut in quarters and serve.

Cheat's easy aubergine Parmigiana

Gently fry aubergine slices (cut lengthways into long pieces 1cm thick) in olive oil until soft. Drain on kitchen towel. Meanwhile, make a tomato sauce with fried onions, garlic, tomato passata and olive oil, and allow to reduce slightly. Put a layer of the aubergine on the bottom of a baking dish, follow with a layer of sauce and then a layer of hunks of fresh mozzarella and a scattering of basil and black pepper. Continue, finishing with a layer of cheese. Grate over some Parmesan and cook in a hot oven for 20 or so minutes until the cheese has browned on top.

Valentine Warner

Valentine Warner dropped out of art college to learn to cook, and has worked for chefs such as Alastair Little and Rose Carrarini as well as starting a catering company. In 2008 his first TV series *What to Eat Now* was aired, and he's now written several books to accompany the show. This recipe is from *What to Eat Now – Spring & Summer*.

Breakfast rhubarb with ginger

My fried breakfast programming is broken with a flash of electric pink when the spring rhubarb session starts. Ginger and rhubarb were born to be lovers. I like this with goat's yoghurt.

serves 4
7 medium stems of fresh rhubarb
a thumb-sized piece of fresh root ginger
4 tbs runny honey
freshly squeezed juice of ½ an orange
yoghurt, to serve

Trim the rhubarb and rinse it in cold water – the little beads of water that cling on and the orange juice are all you need to poach the stems perfectly. Cut each rhubarb stem into 6 lengths and put in a saucepan. Peel and finely slice the ginger (if cut too large it is not pleasant to eat and will end up in the bin). Add the ginger to the rhubarb. Drizzle with the honey and pour over the orange juice.

Cover the pan and cook over a low heat for about 10 minutes until the rhubarb is tender but not breaking apart; a sharp knife inserted into one of the pieces should slide in with no resistance. Don't be tempted to stir or prod the rhubarb as it cooks or it will quickly turn to mush – just give the pan a shake now and then.

Remove the pan from the heat and, using a slotted spoon, carefully transfer the rhubarb to a small serving dish. Return the pan to the heat, bring to the boil, and cook for 3–4 minutes until syrupy. Allow to cool. Pour the sauce over the rhubarb and serve with lots of yoghurt.

I love **tinned beef consommé** – it's excellent in stews and great for depth – 20,000 leagues to be precise.

Skye Gyngell

Skye Gyngell is head chef at Petersham Nurseries Café in Surrey, where she serves delicious seasonal food. She was born in Australia and has worked as a chef in Paris, London and Sydney. Her two cookbooks, *A Year in My Kitchen* and *My Favourite Ingredients*, have won a clutch of awards.

Warm chocolate puddings

These comforting little treats literally ooze chocolate from their centre. Gooey and molten, they are wonderful simply served with cream. I also like them with coffee ice cream, or cream flavoured with a touch of honey.

serves 6

150g unsalted butter, plus extra to grease
300g good-quality dark chocolate (minimum 64% cocoa solids)
4 organic free-range eggs
3 organic free-range egg yolks
50g plain flour
150g caster sugar

Lightly butter 6 individual pudding moulds, 200ml capacity. Using a sharp knife, chop the chocolate into 2cm chunks. Melt the chocolate and butter together in a heatproof bowl set over a pan of gently simmering water, then remove from the heat and leave to cool slightly.

Meanwhile, using an electric mixer, beat together the whole eggs, egg yolks and sugar until pale and mousse-like. This will take about 5 minutes – the beaters should leave a ribbon-like trail on the surface of the mixture as you lift them.

Now gently and carefully pour in the chocolate, folding it in lightly but thoroughly to combine. Sift the flour from a good height over the surface and fold in carefully. Spoon the mixture into the prepared moulds and place in the fridge for an hour.

Preheat the oven to 200°C/gas 6. Stand the moulds on a baking tray and bake in the oven for 18 minutes or until the puddings are puffed up with a slight crust. Serve immediately . . . they will smell and taste delicious.

(This recipe is from *A Year in My Kitchen*.)

May

New potatoes and asparagus are good this month, along with radishes, rhubarb and spinach. Towards the end of the month, outdoor-reared, grass-fed spring lambs are at their best, as well as sorrel and rocket.

This is the month to experiment with the new season's potatoes – try them roasted, or in Valentine Warner's favourite salad. Once spring lamb arrives, feast yourself on that, and if you've got a sweet tooth, finish off with Angela Hartnett's semifreddo or a lovely lemon tart.

Antonio Carluccio

Antonio Carluccio OBE was born on the Amalfi coast and came to England in 1975, originally as a wine merchant. He took over the Neal Street Restaurant in 1981 and in 1998 started the first Carluccio's Caffè. A regular on British TV, he has written 13 brilliant books on Italian cooking. The latest is *Antonio Carluccio's Simple Cooking*, which this recipe is taken from.

Stuffed lamb cutlets

For this the lamb cutlets have to be larger than usual, so that they can be stuffed. Get the butcher to cut eight cutlets on the bone, of 2.5–3cm thickness (which means a double cutlet, with the meat of two bones, one of the bones removed).

serves 4
8 large (double) lamb cutlets, French trimmed, fat removed
2 slices of Parma ham or speck, fat removed
8 sage leaves
8 small pieces of fontina cheese, sliced
2 eggs, beaten with salt and pepper
about 6 tbs dried white breadcrumbs
olive oil, for shallow frying

With a sharp pointed knife, make an incision in the flesh of each cutlet, in the side opposite the bone, to make a pocket. Stuff the pockets with the ham, sage and cheese. Press the sides together to seal the cutlets. Dip the cutlets in the egg first, then coat well with the breadcrumbs.

Pour enough olive oil into a large frying pan to cover the base generously and heat gently. Fry the cutlets until brown, about 5–6 minutes per side if you like them juicy, as I do. Drain on kitchen paper and serve.

4 good things to do with new potatoes

Garlic roasted

Fry new potatoes, cut in half, in a frying pan, with a generous splash of vegetable oil. Add 6–7 (or more to taste) whole garlic cloves that you have smashed a bit with a pestle or rolling pin and a sprig or two of thyme or rosemary, plus some coarse black pepper. Colour the potatoes and then tip the whole lot into a roasting tray and roast in the oven until the potatoes are cooked through and crispy on the outside – around 25 minutes.

Roast potato salad

Let the potatoes (left) cool slightly and toss together with some sturdy salad leaves – lollo rosso or romaine or baby gem work well – and some cucumber. Dress with Anissa Helou's tzatziki (page 173) or some some Greek yoghurt and good olive oil. You could also add some chunks of cooked chorizo or leftover chicken.

Watercress potato salad

Whisk together olive oil and white wine vinegar and add a finely chopped shallot to this mix to make a dressing. Toss cooked, warm new potatoes in this, with a scattering of chopped chives, and leave for a couple of minutes for the sharp dressing to soak into the potatoes. Finish with a couple of handfuls of watercress leaves and stir through. Serve immediately.

Spicy new potatoes

A good way to use up leftover potatoes of any kind: fry cooked potatoes in a little oil until just beginning to colour. Turn the heat down, add a sliced onion and fry gently until the onion is translucent. Add a squirt of tomato purée and allow to cook for a couple of minutes. Add a crumbled dried chilli or chilli flakes (to taste), a tsp of smoked paprika (optional) and a crushed clove of garlic (also optional). Cook gently for a further couple of minutes, allowing the flavours to mingle and stirring to avoid catching. Add a splash of water every now and then if the pan gets really dry. Eat.

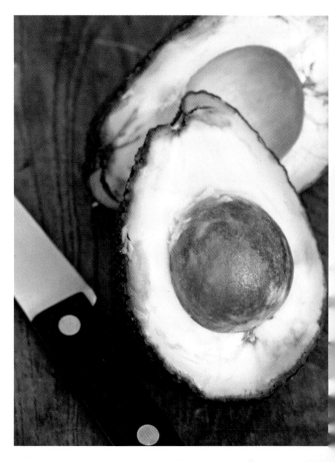

Gordon Ramsay
Mackerel pâté

With four children we always include a few tubs of dips and dunkers when we go out on a picnic – they're easy to prepare, nourishing and travel well. Mix flaked smoked mackerel, crème fraiche, lemon juice and a good dash of horseradish. Then pack a mixture of raw vegetable sticks, cooked shelled prawns tossed in olive oil and some grissini.

Anthony Demetre
English asparagus with chopped poached egg vinaigrette

Cook 2 bunches of asparagus in plenty of salted, boiling water and then refresh in iced water. Set aside. Poach 4 eggs, cooking slightly longer than you would normally – you don't want the yolk too runny but equally not hard. Crush the eggs with a fork, add 1 small finely chopped shallot, 1 tbs each of finely chopped parsley and finely chopped gherkins and the same of miniature capers, and bind with good quality olive oil. Season with salt and pepper.

John Torode
Mufelatta

Take a round cob of bread. Cut in half. Hollow out one half and fill with mozzarella, tomatoes, pesto, pastrami and Mrs Elswood's pickles. Stack them in layers (I aim for three) so you get an even mix. Top with the other half of the bread and push together. Wrap in a tea towel and put a brick on top to really squish it together. When you're ready, remove tea towel and cut into wedges.

Andrew Turner
Avocado with smoked duck

Cut a ripe avocado in half (remove the stone) and remove the flesh, leaving the skin intact. Dice the flesh into cubes and add a squeeze of lemon juice. Then add chopped sun-dried tomatoes, thin strips of smoked duck and plenty of chopped fresh mint and parsley. Place back in the skin and serve with a crisp Riesling.

Mark Sargeant

Mark Sargeant is probably best known for his work with Gordon Ramsay, for whom he worked for 13 years, latterly holding a Michelin star at Claridges. He left Gordon Ramsay Holdings in 2009. He has co-authored several cookbooks with Ramsay and has appeared on various programmes with him, as well as *The Great British Menu*. He is now creative director at the Swan Collection of restaurants in London and Kent.

Rump of new season lamb with grilled asparagus and pea shoot salad

serves 4

4 rumps of lamb
1 tin of anchovies, drained
4 sprigs of rosemary, approx 6cm long, plus extra for roasting
3–4 cloves of garlic, sliced
sea salt and freshly ground black pepper
olive oil

24 asparagus spears, hard parts of the stalks removed
bowl of iced water
olive oil
pea shoots to garnish
juice of ½ a lemon
1½ tbs balsamic vinegar
1–2 large tsp grain mustard

Preheat the oven to 200°C/gas 6. Use a sharp knife to make an incision right the way through each rump and use your finger to open it up a little, then score the fat with a knife. Lay 3–4 anchovy fillets, slightly overlapping each other, on the chopping board. Place a sprig of rosemary on top and gently roll up the anchovy fillets. Repeat with the other sprigs of rosemary. Insert the rosemary into the incisions in the lamb and follow with a few slices of the garlic.

Season the rumps, making sure to rub the salt well into the scored fat. Heat some olive oil in a hot pan and sear the lamb rumps on all sides, scatter in a few extra sprigs of rosemary, 3–4 anchovy fillets and any leftover garlic and bake in the oven for 12–14 minutes until just cooked. Then remove from the baking tray and allow to rest.

For the asparagus, bring a pan of salted water to the boil. Add the asparagus to the water and blanch briefly. Using tongs or a slotted spoon, remove the asparagus from the pan and place immediately into the iced water, then drain. Heat a griddle pan until very hot. Drizzle olive oil over the asparagus and place onto the griddle. Cook, turning occasionally, until nicely marked and browned on all sides. Divide the asparagus onto 4 warmed plates. Slice each lamb rump in half and place these on top of the asparagus, then scatter the plate with the pea shoots. Place the pan from the lamb back on the heat and warm up any juices. Add the lemon juice, balsamic vinegar and mustard and then spoon this over the lamb and asparagus.

Valentine Warner

Potato salad with quails' eggs, capers and anchovies

Any small waxy potatoes, my favourite variety being the pink fir apple, are the only entrants for this recipe. The others can go boil their heads.

serves 6

750g new season's small waxy potatoes, such as pink fir apple or Charlotte, well scrubbed
12 quails' eggs
½ a small red onion
3 sprigs of tarragon
a small handful of chives
a handful of fresh, young parsley leaves
flaked sea salt and ground black pepper

for the mayonnaise:

3 medium free-range egg yolks
1½ tsp Dijon mustard
1 tsp flaked sea salt
a couple of twists of ground black pepper
juice of 1 lemon
50ml olive oil
250ml sunflower oil
5 salted anchovy fillets in oil, drained
2 tbs baby capers, drained

Put the potatoes in a large pan and cover with cold water. Bring to the boil over a high heat, then reduce the heat and simmer for 15–20 minutes or until tender. Drain in a colander under cold running water. Add the quails' eggs to a small pan of cold water, bring to the boil and cook for 2 minutes. Drain in a sieve under running water until cold.

Put the egg yolks, mustard, salt, pepper and lemon juice in a food processor. Turn on the blades and slowly, in a thin, thin stream, pour in the oils. If you find it has become too thick, and there is still oil left, just add a tbs or two of warm water before continuing. If for some reason the mayo splits, do not throw it away, but start again with 1 egg yolk, and slowly pour back in the disaster you created before. Scrape the mayonnaise into a bowl. Roughly chop the anchovy fillets and stir into the mayonnaise with the baby capers.

Slice the potatoes and tip into a serving bowl, if you have one. Peel the wee quails' eggs, cut in half and add to the potatoes. Chop the red onion very finely and scatter over. Strip the whole tarragon leaves from the stems, chop them and the other herbs. Add to the salad. Spoon the mayonnaise on top of the salad and turn with two large spoons until all is mixed and evenly coated. Season with a little extra salt and a good grind of black pepper. Proudly plonk on the table.

(This recipe is from *What to Eat Now – Spring & Summer*.)

Tristan Welch

Tristan Welch has worked at Le Gavroche and L'Arpège, and in 2000 he won the Award of Excellence from the Academy of Culinary Arts. He also worked at the Box Tree, a Michelin-starred restaurant in Yorkshire, for two years, at the five-star Glenapp Castle in Ayrshire and as head chef at the two-Michelin-starred restaurant Pétrus under Marcus Wareing. He is now head chef at Launceston Place in Kensington.

Baked mackerel with bocconcini mozzarella and beetroot

serves 4
tin foil
greaseproof paper
250g cooked beetroot
125g bocconcini mozzarella
olive oil
balsamic glaze (you can buy this)

Maldon sea salt
freshly milled black pepper
½ a bunch of spring onions, finely sliced
4 large mackerel fillets with the bones removed
1 small bunch of dill

Cut 4 20cm x 20cm squares of tin foil and 4 squares of greaseproof paper the same size and place on top of each other so that you have 4 separate pieces of tin foil with greaseproof paper on top of them.

Cut the beetroot to roughly the same size as the mozzarella, then strain the mozzarella and mix with the beetroot.

Dress the beetroot and mozzarella with the olive oil and balsamic glaze. Season with salt and pepper and add the spring onions.

Divide this mixture between the four pieces of greaseproof and foil, placing the mix in the centre. Season the mackerel fillets on both sides with salt and pepper and then place them on top of the beetroot. Drizzle a little extra olive oil on top.

Seal the parcel by bringing the two corners of the left-hand side together and then doing the same on the right-hand side. Pinch both sides together and then pinch along the top of the parcel, and finally down the sides to seal it. Check that the beetroot is still underneath the mackerel and that the parcel edges are well sealed. You can keep these in the fridge for up to a day.

To cook them, place in a oven set to 180°C/gas 4 for 20–25 minutes. When cooked, open the parcels to serve and finish with some chopped dill. This also works very well on a barbecue – just place the parcels on top of the grill for 15–20 minutes.

TRICKS OF THE TRADE

'Never put a melon in the fridge. It will make everything in there taste of the fruit.'

Michel Roux Jr

David Thompson

Australian chef David Thompson is considered by many to be one of the best chefs cooking Thai food in this country. His Michelin-starred restaurant Nahm at the Halkin in London receives rave reviews, and his encyclopaedic book, *Thai Food* is a foodie favourite.

Geng gari (aromatic vegetable curry)
You can also use cauliflower or cherry tomatoes in this curry.

for the curry paste:
45g dried red chillies (soak the chillies in cold water overnight)
a pinch of salt
50g coriander root (you can substitute with 100g coriander stems if necessary)
100g red Thai shallots
100g garlic
75g turmeric
1 tbs white peppercorns, lightly roasted
15g coriander seed, lightly roasted

for the curry vegetables:
200g Jersey Royal potatoes
1l coconut milk, salted
600g coconut cream plus extra 3 tbs to serve
½ tbs palm sugar
2 tbs light soy sauce or salt to season
100g baby corn
50g deep-fried shallots to serve

Make the curry paste by grinding the chillies to a fine paste with a mortar and pestle and a pinch of salt. Add the coriander roots, then shallots, then garlic and turmeric. Add the remaining roasted spices, ground and sieved.

Peel the potatoes and steep in water for a few hours to remove any excess starch. Simmer in the salted coconut milk until cooked, adding water if more liquid is needed. Drain, keeping the coconut stock.

In a smaller pan, add the coconut cream. Fry the paste in it over a medium heat for not less than 5 minutes, stirring to prevent scorching, until the paste is fragrant with the pepper and coriander seed. Don't worry if the paste has separated or is oily – it is meant to be like that – and it really should sizzle. Season with palm sugar and stir until it has melted into the paste and changed colour, then add the soy sauce or salt.

Simmer for a further minute or so. Add your poached potatoes and baby corn. Make sure that the curry covers the vegetables; if it doesn't, add more poaching liquid to cover. Shake the pot to ensure that everything is incorporated well, but do not use a spoon as this could break up the potatoes. Allow to rest for a few minutes to enable the spices to ripen and the flavours to meld. Bring the curry gently to the boil and check the seasoning: it should taste a little salty, rich from the coconut cream, and spicy. Finish with the 3 tbs coconut cream over the top of the curry and serve sprinkled with deep-fried shallots. This curry is traditionally accompanied by the cucumber relish below.

Ajat dtaeng gwa (cucumber relish)

3 tbs coconut or white vinegar
3 tbs caster sugar
4 tbs water
salt
1 small cucumber, washed, quartered lengthwise and sliced
4 red shallots, finely sliced
2 tbs ginger, julienned
1 fresh small long red chilli, julienned or cut into thin rounds
coriander leaves

Combine the vinegar, sugar, water and salt in a small saucepan and bring to the boil. Remove from the heat when the sugar dissolves. Cool, then strain. It should taste sour and sweet. Mix the remaining ingredients in a serving bowl and add the vinegar and sugar liquid. Serve with curry.

4 good things to do with pulses

Cannellini hummus
Whizz a drained, rinsed can of cannellini beans with a crushed clove of garlic, lemon juice, good olive oil and a little salt, until it's about the texture of traditional hummus. Taste and adjust the oil, salt and lemon if necessary. Smear on toasted bread or pitta. You could add a little natural or Greek yoghurt if you wanted it both sharper and creamier – in which case don't add so much oil or lemon.

Chickpeas with spiced spinach
Heat through a tin of chickpeas, drained and rinsed, in enough water to cover them. In another pan, wilt a bag of spinach in a little butter. Set both aside and in another pan cook down a handful of chopped tomatoes, a crumbled dried chilli, 1 tsp cumin, a pinch of oregano and a chopped clove of garlic in a little olive oil. Add a small splash of white wine here, or a drop of white wine vinegar. Bubble off the alcohol and add the cooked spinach and warm chickpeas, and 1 tsp smoked paprika. Stir well and leave on the heat for a minute or two, until everything is hot. Serve as a side to meat or fish, or with an egg.

Very basic dhal
Boil 250g lentils in a litre of water until cooked (how long will depend on which lentils you use – check the packet and be suspicious of any that say they are 'quick cook'). Meanwhile, fry some cumin seeds in a little oil, then add a chopped onion, a thumb of ginger chopped small, a whole green chilli slit down the middle and some chopped tomatoes. Cook very gently for about 10 minutes, then add a pinch of turmeric, 1 tsp garam masala and the same of ground coriander. Cook extremely gently for another 15 minutes, then stir into the cooked lentils. Taste for seasoning and eat straight away.

Pulse salad
You can make this fresh-tasting, hearty salad with cooked Puy lentils, chickpeas, butter beans or borlotti beans. Chop up a couple of ripe tomatoes, a red onion, a fistful of coriander leaves and twice as much parsley and toss together with a couple of tbs olive oil and a squeeze of lemon. Season and eat immediately. You can experiment with adding chopped red pepper or chilli, dill instead of coriander, lemon zest or feta cheese.

Tom Norrington-Davies

Lamb chops with chickpea purée and flatbread

Grill 3 lamb chops per person while you drain a 400g tin of chickpeas. Dry roast 1 tsp cumin seeds for literally half a minute and pop them in a food processor with the chickpeas, 1 level tbs tomato purée, 3 tbs olive oil and the juice of ½ a lemon. Blitz the mixture. Season the chickpea purée to your liking and serve it with the lamb chops and a flatbread like pitta or naan. A knot of coriander leaves mixed with rocket is optional as a garnish.

Tom Norrington-Davies

Lamb chops with minted new potatoes

Grill 3 lamb chops per person while you cook posh new potatoes (Jersey Royals, Cornish mids or French belle de fontaine are great). Chop a generous bunch of mint with cornichons and a red onion, then dress this modernist mint sauce with a tbs of the cornichon vinegar, 2 tbs olive oil and a really mean pinch of sugar. A meal that has no business being eaten with cutlery.

John Torode

One-pot roast lamb

Thinly slice your potatoes and half as much onion – enough to almost fill your roasting tin. Layer them in the tin with some butter. Stick a cake rack on top and put a seasoned leg of lamb on it. Rub a little olive oil into it. Pour half a mug of water over the potatoes. As the whole thing cooks, the potatoes will cook in the fat and juices from the lamb, making them very tasty.

Tristan Welch

Wood-roasted lamb

Get a roasting joint of lamb from the leg (300–400g). Cut a bulb of garlic in half and sprinkle with salt generously, then rub the cut side of the garlic all over the lamb. Protect the lamb by covering it with sprigs of thyme and rosemary: lay out 6 even pieces of soaking wet butcher's string (long enough to go round the meat), then spread out enough herbs to cover the lamb and tie up. The lamb shouldn't take longer than about 20 minutes to cook if the barbecue is at its hottest – use ash wood if possible. Serve with a chicory salad.

 *Angela Hartnett*

Angela Hartnett MBE works for Gordon Ramsay Holdings, where she holds a Michelin star at Murano, her Italian fine-dining restaurant in Mayfair. She also runs York & Albany by Regent's Park and Cielo in Florida. This recipe is taken from her book *Angela Hartnett's Cucina: Three Generations of Italian Family Cooking*, a collection of recipes from her family and particularly her Italian grandmother.

Chocolate and vanilla semifreddo

This recipe (the Italian version of parfait) originally came from my Auntie Maria's mother-in-law Ilda, and then Maria passed it on to Nonna, who passed it on to Mum, who passed it on to me, so it's a great example of Italian women passing recipes down the generations. Be aware that it does contain uncooked eggs, and make sure you always use fresh organic ones.

serves 6

100g amaretti biscuits
a splash of amaretto liqueur
(Disaronno)
100g dark chocolate (70%
cocoa solids)

4 eggs, separated
100g caster sugar
500ml whipping cream, lightly whipped
1 vanilla pod, slit open and seeds
scraped out

Carefully line the base and sides of a 1 litre plastic container with a large piece of cling film (you must ensure there are no splits or gaps in it). Set aside. Crush the amaretti biscuits in a bowl and stir in a generous splash of the liqueur. Spoon the mixture evenly over the base of the lined container and place in the freezer.

Break up the chocolate and place in a bowl set over a pan of simmering water (taking care that the bottom of the bowl does not actually touch the water). Allow to melt. Once it has melted, remove from the heat and leave to cool a little.

Using an electric whisk, beat the egg yolks with the sugar until pale and thickened.

In a separate bowl, whisk the egg whites to form stiff peaks, then fold them into the yolks and sugar. Divide the mixture equally between 2 bowls. Add the melted chocolate to one bowl and mix well. To the other bowl add the cream, another touch of the liqueur and the vanilla seeds.

Remove the container from the freezer. Pour in the chocolate mixture first. Lightly tap the container on a work surface to level the mixture, then pour the vanilla mixture over the top. Tap gently again to even out. Cover with cling film and return to the freezer overnight to set (it needs to freeze for at least 12 hours). When ready to serve, allow to soften slightly at room temperature, then tip on to a chilled plate and cut into slices with a knife warmed in hot water. Serve immediately.

Matt Gillan

Lemon tart

makes 2 large tarts (halve quantities for 1 tart)

for the pastry:
515g T45 (a fine plain flour)
170g icing sugar
240g butter
zest of 1 lemon
1 vanilla pod
1½ eggs, beaten

for the filling:
12 eggs
540g caster sugar
300g double cream
juice from 8 lemons
zest from 3 lemons

for the egg wash:
2 egg yolks
1 whole egg

Crumb the flour, icing sugar and butter together with your fingers. Add the zest, vanilla and beaten egg. You should have a nice firm dough. Wrap cling film around the dough and rest in the fridge for at least an hour.

To make the filling, whisk the eggs and sugar together, then add the cream and mix for 30 seconds. Add the juice and zest and mix for 30 seconds. Pass through a fine sieve and chill the liquid. Skim the foam from the top about 3 times.

Take the dough out of the fridge and allow the pastry to soften a little, then roll out to ½ cm thick. Line a large (25.5cm) tart case with the pastry, ensuring it is pressed right in to the edges of the case. Blind bake the tart case for 20 minutes at 140°C/gas 1. Remove the weights or baking beans and cook for 2 minutes longer. Egg-wash the tart and cook for 2 minutes. Repeat this process twice.

Leaving the tart case in the oven, pour the tart mix into the case using a jug. Cook the tart for 16–20 minutes at 140°C/gas 1 until the centre still wobbles when you shake it. You may find it needs a couple more minutes.

Remove from the oven and leave to cool for at least 3 hours. This is best served at room temperature with a raspberry sorbet or coulis.

If you find you have a little leftover pastry and filling, you can use them to make a few individual tarts.

My SECRET ingredient

It would have to be **Jerusalem artichokes**. They are so versatile and have a fantastic flavour. I always miss them when they're not in season.

June

Asparagus and new potatoes are still good in June, alongside beetroot, blackcurrants, broad beans, new carrots, cherries, Chinese leaves, courgettes, fennel, gooseberries, green beans grown in tunnels, peppers, strawberries, tomatoes and summer turnips and their tops.

This month, Tom Norrington-Davies has lots of wonderful summery things to do with fish, plus Sam and Eddie Hart have a fantastic, celebratory recipe for whole roast suckling pig, and Hugh Fearnley-Whittingstall shares his recipe for quadruple chocolate chip cookies.

Skye Gyngell

Salad of roasted beetroot, walnuts, watercress and mascarpone

I love the gentle sweetness of beetroot – they taste to me quite simply of the earth from which they have been pulled. This salad makes a good first course or you can serve it as part of a larger spread.

serves 4
12 small beetroot
1 tbs and 2 tsp aged balsamic vinegar
2 tbs olive oil
sea salt and freshly ground black pepper
a generous handful of watercress, trimmed
20 walnuts (if you make this in autumn you can use creamy young 'wet' walnuts in the shell)
160–180g mascarpone
a squeeze of lemon juice
4 tbs walnut oil

Preheat the oven to 180°C/gas 4. Wash the beetroot well to remove any dirt, but leave their skins on. If they have little roots, leave them on too as they create a lovely heap on the plate.

Place the beetroot in a roasting tray and drizzle over 1 tbs balsamic vinegar and the olive oil. Season with salt and pepper and cover the tray tightly with foil. Roast on the middle shelf of the oven for 35 minutes, then remove the foil and cook for a further 15 minutes or until the skins are wrinkly and the beetroot feel tender when pierced with a skewer.

Meanwhile, wash the watercress and pat dry. Crack the walnuts and remove them from their shells. Arrange the watercress and warm beetroot on individual plates. Spoon the mascarpone on top and squeeze over the lemon juice, with a light touch.

Scatter the walnuts over the salad, then drizzle over 2 tsp aged balsamic and the walnut oil. Season with salt and pepper and serve, while the beetroot are still just warm.

(This recipe is from *A Year in my Kitchen*.)

4 good things to do with salmon

Herby fried salmon
Take a generous fillet of salmon per person. Put a little butter into a frying pan and gently fry the fish for a couple of minutes on either side until just slightly golden. Add a big spoonful of crème fraiche to the pan and a handful of chopped, soft green herbs – chives, coriander, parsley or tarragon would be nice – and let bubble for a couple of minutes, until the salmon is cooked and the crème fraiche is saucy. Finish with a grind of pepper and a squeeze of lemon.

Steamed salmon
Steam fillets of salmon in a bamboo steamer: add chunks of lemongrass, slices of ginger, garlic and chilli, sprigs of coriander and a little sea salt. Serve with sticky white coconut rice and splashes of soy sauce.

Quick fish curry
Briefly fry a paste of garlic, ginger, 1 tsp turmeric, 1 tsp crushed coriander seeds, 1 tsp crushed cumin seeds, some red and green chillies (to taste) and 1 tsp tamarind paste (if you have any). Add a grated onion and let sizzle for a minute. You could also add a chopped tomato if you like. Pour over a can of coconut milk and let it bubble away until reduced to a curry-like consistency. Add chunks of salmon and simmer for five minutes or until the salmon is cooked – but not for too long as it will start to fall apart. Add some fresh coriander leaves. Taste and season. Serve with flatbreads like chapattis to dip in the curry.

Salmon parcels with dill
Place a fillet of salmon on a large sheet of baking paper. Put a knob of butter on top of the salmon, a sprig or two of dill (or chop it up and sprinkle over) and then pull up the corners of the paper and splosh over a tbs or 2 of dry white wine or vermouth. Add a little salt and pepper and fold over the edges of the paper to make a sealed parcel. Bake in a medium oven for 8 minutes or until the salmon is cooked. Open the parcel carefully and serve with the winey juices.

Allegra McEvedy

Allegra McEvedy MBE is a chef, food writer and broadcaster. She has worked at restaurants like the Groucho, the River Café and Robert De Niro's Tribeca Grill, and even cooked for President Clinton. In 2003 she co-founded the healthy fast-food chain LEON. She is currently chef-in-residence for the *Guardian*. She has published four books, including *Economy Gastronomy*, which accompanied her TV series of the same name, with a fifth out in 2011.

Steamed trout with lemon rice and sautéed cucumbers

Over recent years I've met the arrival of spring sunshine with a growing passion for lightly cooked cucumbers. Clearly the centrepiece of this dish is supposed to be the elegantly steamed trout, yet somehow for me it's the little cucumber dish on the side that is the perfect matchmaker for fennelly fish and lemony rice. A bit like traditional poached salmon, but a little more of our times.

serves 2
80g butter, softened
20g flat-leaf parsley, roughly chopped
salt and pepper
2 whole, portion-sized trout, heads off
1 lemon
1 bulb of fennel, thinly sliced
150g long grain rice
1 cucumber, peeled
1 tbs dill, chopped
1 tbs crème fraiche

Preheat your oven to 200°C/gas 6. Mix half the butter with the chopped parsley and some salt and pepper. Season your fish inside and out. Zest your lemon, then put the zest to one side and cut 3 slices. Halve them and lay three semicircles inside each trout.

Rip 2 pieces of foil around 40cm square and in the centre of each square roughly smear a quarter of the butter mixture in a fish-shaped line where the trout will go. Lay the fennel on top of the butter, give it a quick season, then sit the trout on the fennel and spread the last of the butter mixture along the top of the fish. Bring the top and bottom edges of the foil up so they meet over the fish and fold them tightly together. Taking one side at a time, fold the edges in so they are sealed and the melted butter won't be able to escape: it doesn't really matter how you do this as long as the packet is sealed so the trout can steam, and you don't lose the herb butter.

Put the foil parcels onto a tray and pop them in the oven for 15 minutes.

In a saucepan good for cooking this amount of rice, melt half of the remaining butter. Note the volume of rice before tipping it in, then give the grains a good roll and coat in the butter. Pour on cold water equal to two and half times the volume of the rice, whack the heat up to high and pop a lid on. Once this comes up to boil, turn the heat down to low and simmer for 15 minutes.

Halve your cucumber lengthways, scoop out the seeds and slice into 2cm thick pieces on the diagonal. In a separate frying pan, starting over a high heat, sauté the cucumber chunks in the last of the butter with a lid on for about 8 minutes, stirring occasionally and dropping the temperature halfway through – keep an eye on them as you don't want them to brown at all but just soften a bit. Once this has happened, turn off the heat and add the dill, crème fraiche and some seasoning.

When the rice is cooked, stir in the lemon zest, the juice of the remaining half of the lemon and a touch of salt, then serve up the parcels to be opened at the table.

El Rey de la Vera smoked paprika is ground capsicum pepper from La Vera, in south-west Spain, and is made using a traditional drying process involving oak smoke. This method was originated by monks in the 15th century, and to this day the region of La Vera is renowned for the quality of this product. It comes in several versions: sweet, bitter-sweet and hot. This is my great get-out-of-jail-free for marinades, barbecues, casseroles and wherever flavour is not forthcoming.

Tom Norrington-Davies

Smoked mackerel with beetroot and horseradish

Flake a pair of smoked mackerel fillets roughly and toss them with cooked beetroot, watercress, sliced shallots and capers. Grate fresh horseradish into a small tub of sour cream and season it with salt and pepper. Serve the salad and the cream with plenty of crusty bread (and a seriously dry cider).

Tom Norrington-Davies

Red mullet with wilted lettuce and fresh peas

Fry a shallot in 2 tbs butter until it is sweet and tender. Throw 2 handfuls of fresh or frozen peas into the same pan and add a good pinch of salt. Add just enough fresh fish or chicken stock (or water) to cover the peas, and cook them until they are very soft and sweet (it might take 20 minutes or half an hour). Pull a gem lettuce apart and chop it roughly. Pick 2 sprigs of mint or basil. Grill 2 gutted and scaled red mullet with a seasoning of salt and plenty of olive oil. When the fish is ready, toss the lettuce and herb of choice into the peas and let them wilt. Serve the fish on top of the peas.

Tom Norrington-Davies

Garlicky prawns, courgettes and beans on toast

Fry a couple of cloves of garlic and a fresh red chilli in 3 tbs olive oil. Throw in a handful of cold-water prawns and 2 diced courgettes or a chopped round of asparagus. Fry them until just tender. Add the drained contents of a can of borlotti or cannellini beans. Season with plenty more olive oil and a little salt. Serve this dish on toast or fold in cooked new potatoes.

Tom Norrington-Davies

Hot-smoked fish salad with hazelnuts

Toss hot smoked trout or salmon with an avocado pear, 2 heads of little gem lettuce, a generous handful of roasted, skinless hazelnuts and your favourite vinaigrette. Garnish with chervil or flat-leaf parsley.

TRICKS OF THE TRADE

'When cooking a new recipe, close your eyes and cook the dish from scratch in your mind. This will always throw up a couple of questions that you can solve "virtually" instead of making a costly mistake with your carefully bought ingredients.'

Chris Galvin

Jeremy Lee

Jeremy Lee is from Scotland. His first catering job was as a waiter, but he quickly decided he preferred working in the kitchen. In London he worked for Simon Hopkinson at Bibendum before becoming head chef at the Frith Street Restaurant. In 1994 he launched Euphorium in Islington and the next year took his current position at the Blueprint Café at the Design Museum on the South Bank, where he is head chef.

A tian of tomatoes, courgettes and red chillies

Of course the debate here is about heat, and all chillies have their winning ways, or not. Needless to say, the bold will apply the tip of their finger to the tip of their tongue and cluck with satisfaction if the result is fiery enough. Too hot, though, will diminish the other flavours, so a larger mild chilli is preferable here. This tian is very good eaten as a dish in its own right or as an excellent accompaniment to fish, lightly grilled lamb or very good pork.

serves 4–6
100ml good olive oil, plus extra for brushing dish
4 small onions
2 cloves of garlic
2 sprigs of thyme

2 mild red chillies
1kg plump ripe tomatoes
1kg small courgettes
30g coarse white breadcrumbs
30g Parmesan, grated

Warm the oven to 180°C/gas 4. Take a round earthenware or cast iron gratin dish. Lightly brush the inside of the dish with olive oil.

Peel the onions and the garlic and chop them very finely. Heat a frying pan and pour in the olive oil. Tip in the onions and garlic, along with the thyme, and let cook gently for half an hour or so until soft and lightly coloured. Chop the chillies finely and add to the pan, taking care to remove as many seeds as possible and not touching any part of yourself that may cause regret.

Spoon the cooked onion into the gratin dish and spread. Wash the tomatoes and courgettes well, then slice them and lay them alternately on the onion and garlic mixture. Once done, lightly brush with olive oil, strew with sea salt and grind over some coarse black pepper. Place the tian in the middle of the oven and bake gently for 30 minutes or so until the vegetables are soft. Then add the breadcrumbs and Parmesan and bake for a further 10 minutes until nicely browned. Remove from the oven. A happy thought is that this dish sits very, very well and does not need to be eaten hot. In truth, it is better by far eaten just warm, after the dish has settled.

Jeremy Lee
A warm salad of gooseberries and mackerel

A lovely way to enjoy both of these ridiculously underestimated foods. They work very well together indeed. I have always liked Jane Grigson's heretical suggestion of using a commercial horseradish cream for this recipe. Well, horseradish root remains rare, even today.

serves 4
30g unsalted butter
300g gooseberries
50ml white wine
50g caster sugar
1 heaped tbs horseradish cream
4 spanking fresh mackerel, gutted, cleaned and fins removed
olive oil
sea salt
a fully charged pepper mill
2 lemons

Melt the butter in a pan, then add the gooseberries, wine and sugar. Bring this to a boil, then simmer for 25 minutes or so until all trace of wateriness is banished and the sauce has thickened. Press the sauce through a sieve and let cool, then add the horseradish cream. Cover and put to one side in a pretty bowl.

Heat a ridged griddle pan over a gentle flame. Lightly oil the mackerel, then evenly and lightly season with sea salt. Lay upon the grill and resist the temptation to peek beneath the tail to monitor the progress made. Bravery is required to achieve the blistered charred crust that is such a prize of grilling mackerel. After 7–8 minutes, gently lift the fish from the tail and flip over to grill the other side. Let cook, once again undisturbed, for a further 6–7 minutes. Remove to plates and serve with freshly cut halves of lemon. Grind pepper over and take to the table along with the bowl of gooseberry sauce. A bowl each of little boiled potatoes and a green salad would accompany this well.

Stuart Gillies

Asparagus, feta and smoked salmon salad

Cut raw asparagus thinly at an angle up to the tip, then mix with crumbled feta cheese, cooked chilled peas and broad beans, watercress leaves and a white wine vinegar and olive oil vinaigrette. Season with salt and pepper and serve with smoked salmon.

Sally Clarke

Pasta with summer vegetables, goat's cheese and chives

Cook your favourite pasta, and when it is almost ready add freshly podded peas, fava beans, thinly sliced runner beans and thinly sliced summer carrots. Strain and immediately put back over the heat with a splash of the best olive oil, sea salt, cracked pepper, small pieces of fresh goat's cheese and chopped chives or chervil. Stir briefly together.

Jeremy Lee

Asparagus and fried egg on toast

Boil some asparagus spears and lay on grilled, buttered bread with a fried egg atop; grated Parmesan is a welcome addition.

Henry Harris

Baked fennel with harissa

Toss wedges of fennel in a mixture of Greek yoghurt and rose harissa. Drizzle with olive oil and bake in the oven or in open foil in a kettle barbecue.

Thomasina Miers

Thomasina Miers started cooking aged seven, and is a one-time *Masterchef* winner turned restaurateur who co-owns the brilliant Mexican restaurant chain Wahaca. She is the author of several books, her latest being *Mexican Food Made Simple*.

Chilled cucumber and potato soup

serves 2

1 medium onion
2 large potatoes
olive oil
1 clove of garlic, chopped
2 cucumbers, peeled and diced

Chop and then gently cook the onions and potato in lots of olive oil until the onions go translucent. Add the garlic and the cucumbers. Whizz up, chill and serve ice cold for a delicious summer starter.

My SECRET ingredient

Sabores Aztecas' Mole Rojo sauce is great when I get a craving and don't have time to make my own Mexican mole, particularly when served with some chipotles from the Cool Chile Company.

Sam and Eddie Hart

Brothers Sam and Eddie Hart own and run successful restaurants Fino, Barrafina and Quo Vadis in London, and are the authors of *Modern Spanish Cooking*. Staying at their mother's house in Mallorca has informed much of their cookery, as has travelling and living abroad in Barcelona, Madrid and Mexico City, where Sam ran a nightclub when he was just 22.

Whole roast suckling pig

There is nothing quite like a whole suckling pig for a special occasion. If after the initial 2 hours' cooking the pig is not perfectly crisp, return it to the oven until it is. If you allow 3 hours to cook the pig and it actually cooks in 2¹/₂ , it will happily rest in a warm place until you are ready to eat.

serves 10–12
5–6kg suckling pig
2 heads of garlic
2 shallots
2 dried red peppers
5 sprigs of thyme
5 bay leaves
2 sliced lemons
olive oil
salt and pepper

Preheat the oven to 180°C/gas 4.

On a large board, splay the pig flat so that its legs stick out at the side. Push down on the backbone to open up the ribcage and flatten it down onto the board. If the pig is too big to fit in one roasting tray, cut it in half horizontally with a sharp, heavy knife. The pig should now fit into two domestic oven dishes.

Pat the pig dry with kitchen roll, then scatter the garlic, shallots, peppers, thyme, bay leaves and lemons in the tray and place the pig on top. Rub it with olive oil, then season well with salt and pepper on all sides. Place in the oven and roast for 1 hour. If using two trays, swap them around and cook for another hour, then swap them over again. Cook for another half an hour. Check the pig – if all the skin is wonderfully crisp and deep brown, it is ready.

To carve the pig, first remove the legs and shoulders and carve the meat from them, taking care that each slice of meat has a portion of crisp skin attached. Then carve the meat from the saddle and the ribs, again taking care to keep the skin attached to the meat. If you don't like wobbly bits or are squeamish about what you eat, sprinkle what you have with plenty of salt and serve at once. If you are an offal fan, read on!

Remove the head from the body, then slice it in half lengthways. Inside you will find delicious brain and tongue. The snout, ears and cheeks all make excellent eating as well. Oh, and don't forget the crispy tail!

Sherry is a very Spanish thing and if it's Manzanilla then there's only one place it could have come from. Hildalgo La Gitana happens to be our favourite. It's cool and fresh, it has a decent bite and goes terribly well with ham. This must be served ice cold.

4 good things to do with tomatoes

Tomatoes on toast

Chop up ripe tomatoes, and mix with olive oil, black pepper, salt, a minced clove of garlic or a shallot and some shredded basil leaves. Pile on toast or crusty white bread and eat immediately, before the bread goes soggy.

Tomato tart

Get a packet of decent ready-rolled puff pastry, and lay it out on a buttered or greaseproof-papered baking sheet. Pinch up each corner of the pastry slightly, to make a very shallow ridge around the edge. Cover the pastry in a mixture of halved cherry tomatoes that have been tossed in olive oil and salt and pepper, some hunks of crumbled goat's cheese (or swap the cheese for anchovies) and a very light sprinkling of thyme leaves. Drizzle a little more olive oil and season. Brush the pastry edges with beaten egg (or whatever the packet says) and bake for about 20–25 minutes (or, again, according to the instructions). Eat while warm and crispy.

White fish with olives and tomatoes

Find 4 chunky steaks or fillets of a large white fish and put them in a greased baking dish with lots of small, halved tomatoes (cherry or slightly larger) and stoned, halved black olives, and perhaps some rinsed capers or caperberries if you like them. Add a slosh of white wine and drizzle everything with a little olive oil. Bake in the oven until the fish is cooked through (about 15 mins in a medium oven) and the tomatoes are collapsing. Serve with dippable bread and a green salad.

Tomato and halloumi salad

Halve a mixture of tomatoes (yellow, red and green, preferably) and put in a bowl with a tbs of olive oil. Slice a block of halloumi into 1cm thick pieces, halve each one, then dip in flour and fry in olive oil until golden. Toss the hot cheese with the tomatoes and add a couple of generous handfuls of roughly chopped flat-leaf parsley. Squeeze over a little lemon or lime juice to taste. Serve quickly while the cheese is still crispy outside and warm within.

Hugh Fearnley-Whittingstall

Hugh Fearnley-Whittingstall is a cook and campaigning food writer and broadcaster. He shot to fame with his tremendously successful Dorset-based River Cottage television series and books, and he now has River Cottage Canteens in both Axminster and Bath. He is currently fronting the Landshare campaign, which matches keen growers with spare land.

Quadruple chocolate chip cookies

This is my personal contribution to the pantheon of recipes that help people lose weight. The finished biscuits are about 73 per cent fat free. And of course, like all slimming products, the more you eat, the thinner you get.

100g soft unsalted butter
100g caster sugar
100g soft brown sugar
1 egg
125g self-raising flour
100g ground almonds
50g cocoa powder
50g plain chocolate chips
50g milk chocolate chips
50g white chocolate chips

Cream the butter and both sugars until soft and whippy. Beat in the egg and then mix in the flour, then the ground almonds and cocoa. Mix in the chocolate chips. With floured hands, roll chunks of dough into walnut-sized balls. Place them well-spaced apart (they will spread out a lot) onto greased, floured baking sheets or non-stick parchment. Bake at 180°C/gas 4 for 12–15 minutes, until golden brown. Eat while still warm and soft, or cooled and crispy.

Fish 4 Ever sustainable tinned fish: I'm a big fan of tinned fish, from sardines to mackerel, and it's great to be able to buy it with a clean conscience.

Bill Granger

Strawberry vacherin

serves 8
250g ripe, best quality strawberries
250 caster sugar
4 medium egg whites
a pinch of salt

Preheat the oven to 130°C/gas ½ . Line a baking tray with baking paper. In a bowl, crush 4 or 5 ripe strawberries with 1 tbs sugar, using the back of a fork.

Place the egg whites and salt in a clean, dry, large bowl and whisk until soft peaks form. Add the rest of the sugar gradually, whisking continuously, until the mixture becomes stiff and glossy. Add the crushed strawberry mixture gradually and whisk through.

Spoon the meringue into 8 mounds on the prepared baking tray and bake for 1 ¼ hours. Remove from the oven and allow to cool. (The meringues can be stored in an airtight container for up to a week.)

To serve, scatter with the rest of the strawberries. You could also top each meringue with a scoop of ice cream.

(This recipe is from *Feed Me Now*.)

July

Blackcurrants, broad beans, broccoli, spring cabbage, summer cabbage, carrots, new cauliflower, courgettes, cucumber, fennel, French beans, lettuce, loganberries, redcurrants, strawberries, tayberries, tomatoes and watercress are all good this month.

This month, try Alain Ducasse's rich roast chicken, or Mark Sargeant's pea, broad bean and mint on toast. Have a go at April Bloomfield's zesty Greek salad or Gordon Ramsay's slow-roasted tomatoes.

Antonio Carluccio

Caponata Siciliana (Sicilian vegetable stew)
Versatile, delicious and easy to make, caponata is probably Sicily's best-known dish.

serves 4–6
800g aubergine
1 large onion, peeled and chopped
1 tbs olive oil
3 ripe tomatoes
1 tbs tomato purée, diluted with a little water
1 tbs caster sugar
1 tbs salted capers, soaked
20 green pitted olives
1 tbs white wine vinegar
chopped leaves and stalks of 1 head of celery
1 tbs raisins
salt and pepper
1 tbs pine kernels (optional)

Cut the aubergine into 3cm chunks, soak in cold water for 5 minutes, then drain. This will stop the aubergine from absorbing too much oil.

Fry the onion in the olive oil in a large pan for a few minutes to soften. Put the aubergine chunks into the pan and fry until soft and tender, about 10 minutes. Add the tomatoes, diluted tomato purée, sugar, capers, olives, vinegar, celery leaves and stalks, raisins and some salt and pepper and stew slowly until everything is melted together, about 30 minutes. Stir in the pine kernels, if desired, and serve either cold or warm as a side dish, or by itself with bread.

(This recipe is from *Antonio Carluccio's Simple Cooking*.)

Mitch Tonks

Grilled sardines with walnut and olive salad

Rich oily sardines are wonderful combined with crisp salad ingredients. I particularly like the flavour of the walnuts with the fish, and the olives have a distinct saltiness that seems to bring the whole dish together. Look for sardines which have hues of gun-metal green and purple on their backs and avoid any with red heads or split bellies. Larger sardines which have become pilchards will not be as oily as the smaller fish.

serves 2–3
6 sardines
olive oil
1 tbs dried oregano
1 red onion, finely sliced
6 ripe tomatoes
10 olives, black or green
1 round lettuce
1 cucumber – halved and seeds removed
a small handful of walnuts

for the dressing:
1 egg yolk
½ a clove of garlic
a pinch of oregano
1 tsp Dijon mustard
a good splash of white wine vinegar
1 anchovy fillet
olive oil

Heat a grill pan or a traditional grill until hot. Brush the sardines with oil and some of the oregano and grill skin-side up for 4–5 minutes until crisp and cooked.

To make the dressing, place the egg yolk in a small food processor with the garlic, oregano, mustard, vinegar and anchovy and blitz, gradually add oil until thickened, then loosen with a splash of water until at pouring consistency. Taste and season – Worcestershire sauce is a great addition if you fancy.

Simply mix together all the remaining salad ingredients, season with salt, then toss with the dressing and lay the sardines on top of the salad or break up and toss through it.

(This recipe is from *Fish*.)

Salted capers: I love to eat them in salads, with fish, with cured meats on toast with tomatoes, mixed with olives, in relishes . . . Love the saltiness.

Gordon Ramsay
Slow-roasted tomatoes

We go mad whenever English tomatoes are in season; the kitchens are filled with so many that we could probably fill a bathtub with them. Slow-roasting is a great way to use them up and intensifies the flavour. Heat the oven to the lowest setting and halve the tomatoes. Arrange them, cut-side up, on a lightly oiled roasting tray and scatter over some chopped garlic, shallots and thyme leaves. Drizzle generously with olive oil and sprinkle with sea salt and freshly ground pepper. Gently roast for an hour until tender. Serve at room temperature with pasta, fish dishes or salads, or as a bruschetta topping.

Henry Harris
Watermelon and feta salad

Toss cubes of watermelon, feta and mint together with a splash of olive oil and a good milling of black pepper.

Thomasina Miers
Cauliflower and green bean salad

Steam cauliflower florets and green beans for 2–3 minutes so that they still have some bite. Toss them into a French dressing with a mashed anchovy fillet and small clove of garlic, Dijon mustard and masses of freshly chopped tarragon.

Giorgio Locatelli
Cipollotto di tropea salad

I'm in love with this salad: just blanch some runner beans in salted water for 3 minutes, add mint leaves and cipollotto di tropea (which is from Calabria and is similar to a spring onion), and fresh green almonds.

4 good things to do with tofu

Stir-fried tofu

Cut firm tofu into bite-sized chunks and fry gently in vegetable or peanut oil until golden – don't move around too roughly or it will break up. Turn up the heat and add spring onions, strips of carrots, sliced pak choi or Chinese cabbage and stir briefly. Add a little soy sauce, some sweet chilli sauce if you like, or sliced red chilli, and some unsalted peanuts which you've smashed up a bit and toasted lightly. Stir in some ready cooked noodles. Eat while hot and slippery.

Lime and coriander tofu

Dust thick slices of firm tofu in flour and fry gently in vegetable oil until golden. Mix a couple of handfuls of roughly chopped coriander with the juice of a whole lime, an equal amount of olive oil, $\frac{1}{2}$ a crushed clove of garlic and a little salt and pepper. Douse the hot tofu in the zingy dressing.

Watercress salad

Gently fry cubes of tofu dusted in seasoned flour. Mix into a salad of watercress, sliced red onions, strips of cucumber and avocado. Dress with soy sauce and groundnut oil or sweet chilli sauce.

Peas and broccoli

Break broccoli into florets and stir-fry with cubes of tofu and a handful of peas and 2 more of spinach. Sprinkle with a little splash of fish sauce and some soy sauce, allow to cook briefly and serve as a side.

Mark Sargeant

Peas, broad beans and pecorino on toast

serves 2 as a main course or 4 as a starter

150g peas
250g broad beans
a small bunch of fresh mint, leaves picked
50g finely grated fresh pecorino cheese, plus extra for serving
1 tbs mascarpone
sea salt and freshly ground black pepper
juice of 1 lemon
extra-virgin olive oil
4 slices of sourdough bread
4 small balls of buffalo mozzarella cheese
a handful of pea shoots

Put the peas, broad beans, mint, pecorino, mascarpone, salt, pepper and lemon juice into a blender and pulse it a few times to break the mixture down to a rough purée. Scrape the mix into a bowl and drizzle in a little olive oil to loosen it up and give it body.

Put the mixture into the fridge to chill, while you grill or toast the bread. Remove the mix and spread thickly onto the toast, then tear the mozzarella on top. Grate some more pecorino over and drizzle with a little more oil. Garnish with pea shoots and serve.

Alain Ducasse

Alain Ducasse, from south-west France, is one of the most famous chefs of his generation, and currently holds 20 Michelin stars around the world, as well as running three restaurants that each have three Michelin stars in Monaco, Paris and London. He has mentored a huge number of chefs and is incredibly committed to teaching and innovating in food. This is one of his favourite family recipes.

Grandma Jeanne's roast chicken

serves 4
1 whole head of garlic
4 large red onions
1 free-range chicken from Les Landes (a region in south-west France)
3 tbs goose fat
salt

Heat the oven to 180°C/gas 4. Separate the garlic cloves and peel away the skin, leaving the last layer. Peel the onions and cut into quarters. Salt the skin and interior of the chicken. Stuff the chicken with the garlic cloves. Grease the skin of the chicken with the goose fat.

Place the chicken in an oven dish, laying it on its side (so the legs are top and bottom). Surround the chicken with the onions. Place the chicken in the oven and cook for 1 hour and 30 minutes.

The key to this dish is the position of the chicken during cooking. By placing the chicken in this way, it keeps the breast meat tender and mellow.

Simply extra-virgin olive oil.

Sanjay Dwivedi

Sanjay Dwivedi is from India and his food is influenced both by his homeland and by his French cookery training. He has worked all over the world, from Tantra in LA to Tabla in New York, and was even a personal chef to the Rolling Stones. Since 1999 his restaurant Zaika in London has been serving his delicious takes on classic Indian dishes.

Green herb chicken tikka

This is a very simple dish. It's great for the barbecue and can be prepared two days in advance. It is best served with a glass of chilled Sauvignon Blanc from New Zealand.

serves 4
4 organic chicken breasts, cut into 4cm cubes

for the first marinade:
10g peeled ginger
10g peeled garlic
juice of ½ a lemon
salt (to taste)

for the second marinade:
70g thick natural yoghurt
2 cloves of garlic
1 medium-sized green chilli
40g coriander leaves, chopped
20g mint leaves, chopped
20g basil
20g rosemary, leaves picked
10g garam masala powder
juice of ½ a lemon
salt (to taste)
20ml olive oil

For the first marinade, purée the ginger and garlic to a paste and rub into the chicken cubes, then add the lemon juice and salt. Leave for 30 minutes.

For the second marinade, put all the ingredients in a liquidiser and blend to a fine paste. Rub the new marinade into the chicken and leave to marinate for at least 6 hours or overnight.

Finally, skewer and cook in a very hot oven at 200°C/gas 6, or on the barbecue, and serve with a fresh, green salad.

My SECRET ingredient

Maggi coconut milk powder is the best substitute for coconut milk, if fresh is not available. As it's in powder form you can control the thickness, and tinned coconut milk can sometimes give a tinny taste. I use it for just about anything: instead of cream in a dessert, or if I'm making a starter or main course I'll add a couple of chillies to it to counterbalance the sweetness.

Tom Norrington-Davies
Sardines on toast

Grill 3 or 4 fresh, gutted sardines per person. Chop the ripest, sweetest tomatoes you can get hold of with a handful of black olives, 2 cloves of garlic, a small bunch of basil and a red onion. Season the chopped tomatoes with olive oil and a splash of vinegar. Divide the salad among slices of grilled bread. Serve the sardines on top of the tomatoey bread.

Tom Norrington-Davies
Pork chops with broad beans

Rub 2 pork chops with a marinade made from $\frac{1}{2}$ tsp smoked paprika, 1 tsp tomato purée, 1 tbs runny honey, 1 tbs posh(ish) vinegar, $\frac{1}{2}$ tsp salt and enough mild olive oil to loosen everything up. Fry the chops until done to your liking and let them rest. Meanwhile, boil 2 handfuls of freshly shucked broad beans for 5 minutes. Drain them and toss them with the juices of the rested chops. Throw the beans over the chops and eat this very loose-limbed supper with your fingers. Mop up juices with sourdough bread.

Tom Norrington-Davies
Crab with chips and mayonnaise

If you are a fan of oven chips and mayonnaise, buy a fresh crab – 700g (a one-and-a-half-pounder, in fishmonger speak) is a perfect portion. Boil it in plenty of salted water for 8 minutes, and as soon as it is cool enough to handle, spend a lazy lunchtime picking over and eating it with the above.

Tom Norrington-Davies
Mackerel with broccoli and spicy anchovy sauce

Grill 2 portion-sized mackerel for 3 minutes on either side and season them with sea salt and olive oil. Let them rest and break a head of broccoli into bite-sized florets. While you steam the broccoli, chop 3 anchovy fillets, 2 cloves of garlic and 1 red chilli to a near-paste. Melt the paste in a small frying pan with 2 tbs butter. Toss it with the warm broccoli. Serve the broccoli next to the mackerel.

TRICKS OF THE TRADE

'Always make sure that meat or fish has been dried
with a kitchen towel. If it is wet it can stick in
the pan and won't colour evenly and, of course,
it will take longer.'

Martin Nisbet

FRESH GuiltHEAD BREAM
£ 2·95 lb
£ 6·49 kg

SH RED BREAM
2·50 lb
5·51 kg

FRESH MACKERAL
£ 1·99 lb
£ 2·39 KG

4 good things to do with courgettes

Feta and potato cakes

Grate a courgette with a couple of potatoes and mix with a beaten egg and some crumbled feta cheese and chopped parsley. Shape into flat wide cakes and chill for a few minutes in the fridge, then dust with flour and fry very gently and slowly until nicely browned and the potato is cooked through.

On toast

Chop up courgettes and cook slowly with olive oil or butter with a squeeze of lemon until really soft. Add basil and mint leaves, torn up, season and pile up on hot toast, or stir into pasta.

Creamy pasta

Cook several chopped courgettes slowly in a little butter with the leaves stripped from a sprig of thyme. After 15 minutes or so, stir through a dollop of crème fraiche, cream or even a creamy natural yoghurt. Use as a sauce for ready-made stuffed pasta – spinach and ricotta tortellini would be nice – and grind over plenty of pepper.

Courgette salad

Using a potato peeler, cut thin strips of raw courgette from top to bottom. Season and dress with lemon juice and olive oil and add to any salad.

April Bloomfield

April Bloomfield started her cookery training in Birmingham, then moved to London where she worked at Kensington Place, Bibendum and the River Café. She also worked at Roscoff in Belfast and at Chez Panisse in California, before heading up her own kitchens at the Spotted Pig, the John Dory and the Breslin, which are all in New York.

Greek salad

The key to this salad is the ingredients – they have to be fresh and crisp. I buy mine at the local farmers' market on the way to work. The tomatoes should have a good balance between sweet and tart – I love Green Zebras, but use whichever variety you like best.

serves 4
for the vinaigrette:
4 tbs sherry vinegar
1 tsp salt
2 large spring onions
4 tbs olive oil

for the salad:
1 medium cucumber
16 golf-ball-sized tomatoes
½ a lemon
olive oil, for drizzling
20 olives, ideally taggiasca or niçoise
2 sprigs of mint, leaves picked
175g feta, roughly crumbled

Place the vinegar in a bowl and add the salt. Slice the spring onions diagonally into ½ cm slices, using both white and green parts. Add them and the olive oil to the vinegar and allow to sit for five minutes.

Wash and dry the cucumber and tomatoes. Peel the cucumber, then chop it and the tomatoes into rustic bite-sized pieces. Lay on a tray and season evenly. Squeeze the lemon over the top, then drizzle with a little olive oil. To serve, divide the cucumbers and tomatoes between four plates, or place everything on a platter. Stir the vinaigrette and pour it on top, making sure it is evenly distributed. Arrange 5 olives on each plate, then scatter over the whole mint leaves and feta.

Claude Bosi
Strawberries with hibiscus

Roughly chop 500g English strawberries. In a pan, heat 300ml water and add 150g sugar. Allow to cool until tepid, then add a grated vanilla pod and bring to the boil to infuse. Add the strawberries, and leave to soak for 20 minutes. Make a pot of hibiscus-flower tea and leave to cool. Remove strawberries from the stock and place in bowls or medium-sized ramekins. Top with the cool hibiscus tea (to create a consommé effect) and serve with a good dollop of clotted cream and/or chunky shortbread biscuits.

Michael Caines
Strawberries with balsamic and mint

Quarter some strawberries and sprinkle them with sugar. Crush half of the strawberries with a fork to extract all their juices. Mix all the strawberries together with some freshly chopped mint and leave to marinate for half an hour. Serve with a drizzle of aged balsamic vinegar and vanilla ice cream.

Tom Aikens
Poached strawberries with mint

You could take this on a picnic, in which case it has to be prepared in the morning. Split and scrape two vanilla beans and add them to a pan containing about 600ml water. Mix in 200g caster sugar and the juice of a lemon and bring to a gentle simmer. Cook for 5 minutes and then add a generous kilo of strawberries, washed, trimmed and halved. Simmer for a minute more and then remove the pan from the heat and place contents in a cool, metal bowl. Chill in the fridge for a couple of hours. When you're ready to eat, take a handful of chopped mint, a small bunch or so, and sprinkle liberally. Serve in bowls.

Jason Atherton
Berries with meringues

Take a punnet each of strawberries, raspberries and blueberries. Boil up some sugar, water with vanilla and star anise and pour it over the berries, then chill and eat with crushed meringues and clotted cream.

August

Aubergines, blueberries, chard, courgettes, fennel, leeks, lettuce, peas, peppers, strawberries and sweetcorn are all good in August. The first apples and Victoria plums also start to appear before the end of the month.

Now is the time to take food outside – take Anissa Helou's fantastic hummus and tzatziki on a picnic, or pack Bryn Williams's wonderfully fresh raw courgette salad. Go for Thomasina Miers's sticky Mexican ribs, or try Oliver Peyton's traffic-light-coloured jellies on a sunny afternoon.

Anissa Helou

Anissa Helou was born in Lebanon, and after a successful career in Europe in the art world decided to change course in 1999 and focus on food, especially from the Levant. She has written six acclaimed books and this recipe is taken from the fifth, *Modern Mezze*. She is also a respected journalist and broadcaster and has recently started teaching cookery at Anissa's School in London's Shoreditch.

Hummus and tzatziki

serves 4
for the tzatziki:
4 small Middle Eastern or
1 regular cucumber(s)
sea salt
450g Greek-style yoghurt
1 clove of garlic, peeled and crushed
2–3 tbs chopped dill

for the garnish:
extra-virgin olive oil
paprika for sprinkling
sprigs of dill

for the hummus:
660g jar of chickpeas (425g net weight)
100ml tahini
juice of 1½ lemons, or to taste
1 clove of garlic, peeled and crushed
fine sea salt

for the garnish:
sweet paprika
extra virgin olive oil
1 tbs chopped flat-leaf parsley
(optional)

To make the tzatziki: if using small cucumbers, halve lengthways and slice thinly. If you have a standard cucumber, peel, halve, deseed and grate, then salt lightly. Let sit for about 15 minutes, then squeeze to get rid of excess moisture. Mix the cucumber, yoghurt, garlic and dill together in a bowl. Taste and adjust the salt if necessary. Spoon into a serving dish, drizzle with a little olive oil and sprinkle with a little paprika. Serve garnished with dill.

To make the hummus: drain the chickpeas, rinse well and drain thoroughly. Put them in a food processor with the tahini and lemon juice and process until very smooth. Transfer to a bowl. Add the garlic and salt to taste, mixing well. If the hummus is too thick, add a little more lemon juice, or water if the flavour is already tart enough. Taste and adjust the seasoning.

Spoon the hummus into a serving dish. With the back of the spoon, spread it across the dish, raising it slightly at the edges and in the centre, so that you have a shallow groove in between. Sprinkle a little paprika over the raised edges and drizzle a little olive oil in the groove. Sprinkle with parsley, if using. Serve with pitta bread.

Anjum Anand

North Indian lamb curry

This a typical dish from Punjab and we have been making it at home for as long as I can remember. The whole spices added at the beginning of the recipe bring a wonderful depth and roundness to the flavour of the curry, but if you don't have any, don't worry – the curry is delicious regardless. Eat with roti or rice pilaff or, as we sometimes did, in a hot, buttered baguette – truly delicious.

serves 6–8

25g fresh ginger, peeled
30g garlic (approximately 10 large cloves), peeled
3 tbs vegetable oil
2 each black and green cardamom pods
1 bay leaf
1 large onion, peeled and finely chopped
800g small lamb cubes, with the bone in
1–2 green chillies (optional)
½ tsp turmeric powder
1 tbs coriander powder
1 tsp garam masala
salt, to taste
4 medium tomatoes, puréed
500ml water
a good handful of fresh coriander leaves and stalks, chopped

Make a paste of the ginger and garlic, adding a little water to help if you are using a blender.

Heat the oil in a large non-stick saucepan. Add the cardamom pods and bay leaf and stir for 10 seconds before adding the onion. Fry for about 8 minutes until nicely browned. Add the lamb and stir-fry for 2–3 minutes, then add the ginger and garlic paste, the spices and salt. Cook, stirring, for a couple of minutes until the pan is dry.

Add the tomatoes, bring to the boil, and simmer until the masala has cooked through, around 10–15 minutes. The oil will come out of the masala and there should be no harshness to the flavour. Add the water, bring to a boil, then lower the heat and cook, covered, for 35–45 minutes until the lamb is tender. Stir occasionally and make sure there is always some water in the pan. When cooked, stir in the coriander, turn off the heat and serve.

(This recipe is taken from *Indian Food Made Easy*.)

Bryn Williams
Courgette and pine nut salad

Slice green and yellow courgettes lengthways into ribbons, place strips in a colander and season with a little salt. Leave to stand until the excess water is extracted. Pat courgettes dry with paper towel and place on a plate. Sprinkle with toasted pine nuts and drizzle with balsamic dressing (balsamic vinegar, salt and pepper, olive oil and lemon all whisked together), then add a layer of wild rocket leaves and finish with Parmesan shavings and more of the dressing.

Vivek Singh
Roast bream with green mango and coconut

Blend together half a coconut's flesh and a green mango with an onion, red chilli flakes and some salt and sugar. Add a little oil or water to blend into a coarse paste. This paste can be used either as a chutney or dip on its own, or as a marinade for sea bass, gilt bream or even mackerel. Cook the fish either in an oven or on a barbecue, ideally wrapped in a banana leaf or tin foil with a little oil.

Henry Harris
Garlic sourdough

Grill thick slices of sourdough bread and then rub with a peeled clove of garlic – it acts like a grater – then drizzle with good olive oil and eat, adding slices of prosciutto or a good salami.

Fuchsia Dunlop
Stir-fried cabbage

One of the easiest vegetables to stir-fry is Chinese leaf cabbage. Two methods: 1) Heat oil in a wok, add a couple of dried chillies (cut into sections, deseeded) and 1 tsp whole Sichuan pepper. Sizzle until the chillies are darkening but not burnt, then add sliced Chinese cabbage and stir-fry until succulent but still a little crisp. Salt to taste. 2) Stir-fry your sliced cabbage in a little oil and, when it is nearly done, push it to the side of the wok, tip 1–2 tbs oyster sauce into the space and stir it until it is hot. Then mix the sauce with the cabbage and stir-fry until cooked.

Shane Osborn

Nut-roasted goat's cheese salad with roasted peppers

serves 4
2 red peppers
2 tbs olive oil
salt and pepper
½ tbs chopped walnuts
½ tbs chopped hazelnuts
4 tbs breadcrumbs
1 tbs milk
2 egg yolks
4 slices of goat's cheese or 4 small whole cheeses, approximately 60–80g each
2 tbs plain flour
20 black olives, stoned
100g mixed salad leaves

Preheat the oven to 220°C/gas 7. Cut the peppers in half, remove the seeds and brush the halves with olive oil. Season with salt and pepper and roast in the oven for 15–20 minutes until lightly coloured and softened. Leave to cool and then slice into quarters.

Combine the chopped nuts and breadcrumbs. Add the milk to the eggs yolks and beat (to make an egg wash). Dust the goat's cheese with flour. Dip in the egg wash, and then in the crumb and nut mix. Place on greaseproof paper on a baking tray. Bake for 6–10 minutes, turning occasionally.

To serve, arrange the peppers on a warm plate with the cheese and olives. Dress the salad leaves with some of your favourite vinaigrette and a touch of salt and pepper and serve.

Variation: the addition of a grilled chicken breast makes this a great main course.

Tom Oldroyd

Tom Oldroyd is head chef at London's Polpo, a Venetian-style bacaro restaurant. He has previously worked at Bocca di Lupo with Jacob Kenedy, and at Alastair Little. Russell Norman, the owner of Polpo, was previously at Caprice Holdings.

Risi e bisi (Venetian rice and peas)

serves 6 as a starter or 4 as a main

1kg fresh peas in their pods
2 onions
2l water
70g butter
50ml olive oil
100g pancetta lardons
500g Carnaroli rice
60g Parmesan
a handful of fresh mint, chopped
a handful of fresh parsley, chopped

Shell the peas, and leave the pods to one side. Place the pea pods, 1 onion and water in a pan and simmer to make a stock.

Finely chop 1 onion and sweat in the olive oil and 50g of the butter. Add the pancetta lardons and cook for a few minutes. Add the rice and stir for 2 minutes. Add the fresh peas and half of the stock. Let the rice absorb the liquid, and then stir in the remaining stock. Simmer the rice until al dente Add the Parmesan, remaining butter, mint and parsley. Let it rest for 4 minutes, and then serve.

My SECRET ingredient

I love a tin of sardines in olive oil. Sardines on toast make a perfect breakfast or lunch, so they are perfect to keep in the store cupboard for a quick snack.

Tim Hughes

Scott's is a seafood restaurant in the Caprice group. It has been around since 1851 and on its present site in Mayfair since 1968. It was recently lovingly restored, and this is one of its signature dishes.

Scott's roast cod with Padrón peppers

serves 4
olive oil
2 shallots, diced
1 red chilli, medium heat
100g arancini (white haricot) beans, soaked overnight
salt and pepper
25ml white wine
500ml chicken stock
4 x 180g cod fillet
50g Padrón peppers
80g chorizo, cooked
20g parsley, chopped
garlic

Heat some olive oil in a pan, add the diced shallots and chilli and cook, being careful not to burn the mixture. Drain the arancini beans, add to the pan and sweat down. Season with salt and pepper. Add the white wine and reduce, then add the chicken stock and simmer for 45 minutes or until the beans are cooked. Keep in a warm place.

Heat a non-stick frying pan and add olive oil. Season the cod with salt and pepper and place skin-side down in the pan. Cook until the skin is nice and crispy and the flesh has turned white. Turn the piece of cod over and cook for a further 2 minutes.

Put the Padrón peppers (whole) in a pan with a little olive oil and cook until they start to wilt. Slice the chorizo into 1cm pieces and add to the pan along with the chopped parsley and some garlic if desired. Keep on the heat until the chorizo is hot all the way through.

When ready to serve, spoon the cooked beans onto the middle of 4 plates. Sit the cod on top of the beans and scatter over the Padrón peppers and chorizo.

TRICKS OF THE TRADE

'To make crystal-clear stock, bring the ingredients to the boil, then skim the top and allow the stock to simmer gently. Don't ever allow the stock to boil again as this will boil the fat back in.'

Tom Kitchin

4 good things to do with mackerel

Warm potato salad
Cook small potatoes and, while still warm, toss with smoked mackerel, skinned and flaked, salad leaves and a punchy, mustardy dressing. Eat before the potatoes get cold.

Poached eggs and spinach
Treat smoked mackerel just like smoked haddock – put a fillet (hot or cold) onto a piece of hot, buttered toast with some wilted, buttered spinach and top with a poached egg.

Fishcakes
Make fishcakes with two-thirds cooked, mashed potato to one-third flaked, skinned smoked mackerel and 1 tbs horseradish sauce. Snipped chives, parsley or dill are also an option. Dip in flour, beaten egg and then flour again and cook for about 3 minutes on each side in a frying pan over a medium heat until golden and hot all the way through. Serve with greens and wedges of lemon.

White bean salad
Mix rinsed, drained white beans (butter beans, cannellini or similar) with a finely chopped shallot, flaked, skinned smoked mackerel, a drizzle of olive oil, black pepper and a squeeze of lemon.

Mark Sargeant

Grilled Old Spot pork chops with ratatouille

serves 4

4 tbs olive oil, plus extra for drizzling
3 cloves of garlic, roughly chopped
1kg fresh tomatoes, roughly chopped
2 red onions, cut into about 3cm cubes
3 red peppers, deseeded and cut into about 3cm cubes
2 aubergines, cut into about 3cm cubes
4 courgettes, cut into about 3cm cubes
15g bunch of fresh oregano leaves, roughly chopped
a large bunch of fresh flat-leaf parsley, leaves roughly chopped
4 thick, fatty Old Spot pork chops
salt and pepper

Preheat the oven to 200°C/gas 6. Put the oil, garlic, tomatoes and the vegetables in a roasting tin. Toss together, season and roast for 45 minutes, until tender.

Remove from the oven and mix, breaking down the vegetables slightly. Add the herbs and check the seasoning, then set aside.

Season the pork chops and grill them under a very hot grill, so that the fat crisps up and the chops are golden brown on the outside and just pink in the centre (yes, you can eat pork slightly pink if it's good quality!). This should take about 3 to 4 minutes each side.

Place a good spoon of ratatouille in a bowl and the pork chop on top.

Thomasina Miers

Mexican BBQ ribs

There is something about pork marinated in citrus juices, garlic and chillies and then cooked over hot coals that is totally irresistible. This recipe is inspired by a wonderful lunch I had in Veracruz where they use all these flavours together with herbs and spices to produce a mouth-watering meaty feast. If you can't get the chipotles, which are dried, smoked jalapeño chillies, or the anchos, which have a wonderful sweet flavour, just use a smoky barbecue sauce.

serves 6
3 ancho chillies (optional)
3 tomatoes
3 tbs chipotles en adobo
¼ tsp freshly ground cumin
¼ tsp freshly ground allspice
5 cloves of garlic, coarsely chopped
olive oil
juice of 1 orange
juice of 1 lime
2kg spare ribs

If you are using the anchos, tear out the stems and seeds of these chillies and soak in boiling water for 15–20 minutes to soften them as you would dried mushrooms. Heat a heavy-bottomed frying pan over a high flame and put the tomatoes directly into the pan. Roast for about 10 minutes, turning a couple of times, but otherwise leaving the tomatoes to themselves. They should be blackened and charred in places, to give them a smoky flavour.

Drain the ancho chillies and add them to a blender with the chipotles, spices and garlic. Add the tomatoes, season well with plenty of salt and pepper and blitz to a smooth paste. Wipe the frying pan and put it back over a high flame for a few minutes. Pour in 3 tbs olive oil and when it is hot, turn the heat down to low, add the purée and fry and stir the paste for about five minutes. Add the citrus juices and continue to cook for another 10 minutes. Check for seasoning: you want a well-flavoured marinade.

Marinate the ribs for at least a few hours but preferably overnight. Cook over a medium to hot barbecue for 10–15 minutes or roast in a hot oven (180°C/gas 4) for about 25–30 minutes. Serve with plenty of kitchen paper, as this makes for messy eating!

Thomasina Miers

Succotash salad

Succotash is a salad of summer corn and fresh herbs and, depending on whose recipe it is, green beans, broad beans and tomatoes. This one is flavoured with a tiny amount of the fruity, fiery Scotch Bonnet chilli, mint, fresh herbs and lime, and is delicious with the spare ribs.

1 medium red onion
juice of 2 limes
½ tsp freshly ground cumin
salt and pepper
4 corn on the cob (about 500g corn)
extra-virgin olive oil
3 courgettes, diced
1 Scotch Bonnet chilli, deseeded and finely chopped
2 tsp chopped fresh marjoram (or thyme)
300g cooked black beans, at room temperature
250g cherry tomatoes, quartered
1 large fennel bulb with fronds, chopped
a large handful of mint leaves

Finely chop the red onion and cover half with the lime juice, cumin and plenty of salt and pepper. Run a knife down the length of the corn cobs to shuck the corn, and set aside. Pour a good slug of olive oil in a smoking-hot, heavy-bottomed pan and after a minute add the rest of the onion, courgettes, chilli and marjoram. Season with 1 tsp salt and fry on a high heat for 4–5 minutes until the vegetables have softened a little and coloured. Pour them onto a large plate to cool.

Put the pan back onto heat, add another slug of olive oil and fry the corn over a high heat for a few minutes, seasoning with salt and pepper. Add to the courgettes. Now whisk about 75ml extra-virgin olive oil into the raw red onions and toss through the black beans (rinse them with water if you are buying the ready-cooked ones in cartons), corn, courgettes, tomatoes, fennel and mint leaves, and season the whole lot with salt and pepper to taste. Serve with the spare ribs.

I use masses of **Aspall's Organic Cyder Vinegar** in my Mexican cooking, as it has a much softer flavour than other brands.

4 good things to do with aubergines

Smoky dip

A kind of baba ghanoush: cook a couple of aubergines right in the flame of your gas ring on the hob, or under the hottest possible grill, turning often until they char, blister and burn. When they look completely ruined and your kitchen is smoky, put in a plastic bag for a few minutes to cool and then peel off the blackened skins (this is sometimes easier in running water). With a fork or a blender, mash the flesh with a spoonful of tahini (if you have it) and/or some Greek yoghurt, ½ a clove of garlic, a squeeze of lemon (to taste) and some salt. Eat with pitta or as a dip.

Pine nuts and mozzarella

Toast a couple of tbs pine nuts in a dry pan. Salt, drain and rinse, then grill or fry some long aubergine slices painted with olive oil. Once soft, lay them out flat on a baking sheet. Pile on a layer of mozzarella, pine nuts, a few basil leaves and maybe even some finely chopped tomato. Roll up the aubergine (you may need to secure it with a cocktail stick). Grate over some Parmesan and pop into a hot oven until the mozzarella is oozing out of the side of the rolls, and the Parmesan is golden and bubbling.

Feta and aubergine salad

Gently fry salted, drained and rinsed cubes of aubergine until squishy and golden. Toss the warm cubes with crumbled feta cheese, cherry tomatoes (you could also use roasted tomatoes here), chunks of cucumber and plenty of parsley. Drizzle over a little olive oil. Eat.

With goat's cheese

Fry off some cubes of aubergine, as before. Meanwhile, slowly cook some passata (or tinned tomatoes) with ½ a crushed clove of garlic and a splash of olive oil in a pan. Add the fried aubergines and allow to cook a little longer. Add a handful of spinach to the sauce (optional) and some mild goat's cheese. Stir this through cooked pasta, or pile up on sourdough toast.

Oliver Peyton

Oliver Peyton owns ten restaurants, cafés and bakeries in and around London, including two at the National Gallery on Trafalgar Square. His first cookbook was in collaboration with the gallery and is called *The National Cookbook*. He also owns Inn the Park and the Peyton and Byrne chain. He frequently appears on TV and is one of the judges on *The Great British Menu* series.

Traffic-light jellies

Serve with good local vanilla ice cream. Jelly and ice cream, strawberries and basil: this is my idea of heaven on an English summer's day.

serves 4
for the vanilla jelly (pannacotta):
330ml double cream
50g sugar
1 vanilla pod
1½ gelatine leaves, soaked

for the strawberry jelly:
100g strawberries, sliced
100g caster sugar

330ml water
juice of ½ a lemon
2½ leaves of gelatine, soaked

for the basil jelly:
100g fresh basil
200ml water
30g caster sugar
2½ leaves of gelatine, soaked

To make the vanilla jelly (pannacotta), bring the cream up to a fairly high heat, together with the sugar and vanilla pod, then take off the heat and add the soaked gelatine. Pass through a sieve.

Put the strawberries and sugar into a large bowl, cover with the water, add the lemon juice and cover with cling film. Place the bowl over a pan of simmering water and the strawberries will break down and infuse the water to make a delicious 'strawberry nectar'. Stir in the gelatine.

To make the basil jelly, cook the basil leaves in a large pan of salted boiling water, until soft, then squeeze out and put in a blender with the sugar. Blend to a smooth paste and then add the water. Check for sweetness, then add the gelatine to the basil syrup.

To make a layered jelly using all three, take a glass or plastic mould, and pour in 1cm of the vanilla jelly, or pannacotta, and leave to set in the fridge for a couple of hours. Then make the strawberry jelly and add 1cm of this to the mould. Leave to set again, and then finally make and add 1cm of the basil jelly. You now have a traffic-light-effect three-layered jelly. Serve with ice cream if you wish.

September

Beetroot, blackberries, courgettes, cucumbers, damsons, figs, French beans, curly kale, leeks, lettuce, onions, peaches, early pears, plums, spinach, tomatoes and all of the cabbages are good this month.

This month, try Tom Norrington-Davies's delicious roast quail recipe, or J Sheekey's creamy fish pie. Experiment with cabbage or with Fuchsia Dunlop's lovely chicken salad.

Antonio Carluccio

Trout baked in foil

This cooking method, designed to keep in all the juices and aromas, has been in use since Roman times. Then, they would cook foods enclosed in terracotta, while now we wrap them in foil and oven bake to achieve the same result. So long as the little packages are well sealed, you could also try cooking this on a charcoal grill.

serves 4
4 rainbow trout, about 250g each
32 thin slices of lemon
salt and pepper
1 little bunch of chervil, divided into 4
1 bunch of parsley, divided into 4
100g unsalted butter

Preheat the oven to 200°C/gas 6. Have ready 4 pieces of foil large enough to wrap the fish fairly loosely.

Clean the trout and remove the scales and all the innards (or get your fishmonger to do this). Wash the trout and dry them. Cut off the fins. Make 4 incisions in one side of each fish with a knife.

Arrange the 4 pieces of foil on your work surface, and on each, place 4 slices of lemon. In the cavity of each fish, put some salt and pepper, a quarter of the herbs and 15g butter, cut into small pieces. Close the trout and place each one on top of the lemon slices on the foil, cut side up. Divide the remaining butter, in pieces, between the fish, rubbing into the cuts. Season each fish with salt and pepper, then add another 4 lemon slices to the top of each. Close the foil around each fish to produce a bag.

Bake in the preheated oven for just 20 minutes. The fish are delicious served with a simple boiled potato salad.

(This recipe is from *Antonio Carluccio's Simple Cooking*.)

To be genuine, a ragu for Bolognese should be served with fresh egg tagliatelle.

Tim Hughes

J Sheekey's fish pie

J Sheekey in London started as an oyster bar in 1896. This is one of its most famous dishes.

serves 2
250ml fish stock (a good-quality cube will do)
50ml white wine
125g boneless cod or haddock fillet, skinned and cut into rough 3cm chunks
125g boneless salmon fillet, skinned and cut into rough 3cm chunks
1 tbs chopped parsley

for the sauce:
25g butter
25g flour

90ml double cream
1 tsp English mustard
1 tsp Worcestershire sauce
½ tsp anchovy essence
salt and freshly ground black pepper

for the topping:
20–30g butter
500g floury potatoes, peeled, cooked and mashed
salt and freshly ground white pepper
1 tbs milk
15g fresh white breadcrumbs
10g grated Parmesan

In a large pan, bring the fish stock and white wine to a simmer and poach the fish gently in the liquid for 2 minutes. Drain in a colander over a bowl and leave to cool.

To make the sauce, melt the butter in a thick-bottomed pan over a low heat, then stir in the flour. Gradually add the drained stock and wine mixture, stirring well until it has all been added. Bring to the boil and simmer gently for 30 minutes. Add the double cream and continue to simmer for 10 minutes or so, until the sauce has a thick-coating consistency. Stir in the mustard, Worcestershire sauce and anchovy essence, and season with salt and freshly ground black pepper if necessary. Leave to cool for about 15 minutes.

Gently fold the cooked fish and the parsley into the sauce, and spoon into 2 individual pie dishes or 1 large one, to about 3cm from the top of the dish. Leave to set for about 30 minutes, so that the topping will sit on the sauce when piped over it.

Mix the butter into the mashed potato, season with a little salt and freshly ground white pepper, and add a little milk so that the mixture is soft enough to pipe. Using a piping bag, pipe the potato over the pies in whatever pattern you feel comfortable with. Preheat the oven to 180°C/gas 4 and bake for 30 minutes, then scatter on the breadcrumbs and cheese, and bake for a further 15 minutes until golden.

Rowley Leigh
Peach, tomato and basil salad

Pour boiling water over 6 white peaches and let stand for 10 to 30 seconds, depending on the ripeness of the fruit. Refresh in cold water and skin. Do the same for 6 large tomatoes, which should be firm and full of flavour. Slice the tomatoes thinly and salt them. Cut the peaches into thin segments. Arrange them in an overlapping circle, alternating the two fruits. Squeeze the juice of a lemon over the salad and drizzle lightly with some good oil (very lightly if you are using walnut oil). Tear 6 basil leaves and scatter these over the salad. Mill some black pepper, and serve.

Raymond Blanc
Buttered vegetables

Instead of cooking vegetables in a large pan of boiling water, try using a medium-sized, flat sauté pan with just half a cup of water, a knob of butter and a pinch of salt. Let the vegetables half poach and half steam on full boil. To serve, add some freshly chopped herbs and pour over the cooking juices. Perfect for carrots, asparagus, beans, leeks, cabbage or peas.

Jacob Kenedy
Ginny's pasta with raw tomatoes

From Campania – as made by my beloved grandmother Ginny countless times – is pasta with raw tomatoes. Roughly chop, seeds and all, some ripe, flavoursome tomatoes. Combine with fresh basil and lots of oil, salt and pepper – plus a few black olives if you like – in a large bowl. Cook some long pasta al dente – Ginny uses spaghettini – toss into the sauce, and leave to stand for a minute before serving.

Fuchsia Dunlop
Chinese chicken salad

Tear leftover roast chicken into bite-sized pieces, and mix with salad leaves. Make a dressing to taste from light soy sauce and chilli oil, a dash of black rice vinegar or balsamic, a little sugar to taste and a smidgeon of toasted sesame oil – dilute with a little chicken stock if you have it. Pour over the chicken and toss like a salad. Sometimes I add crushed garlic or ground roasted Sichuan pepper.

Mark Edwards

Mark Edwards started cooking at thirteen, when he took a part-time job in a seafood restaurant in Kent. He has worked in New York, Singapore and Hong Kong as well as in the UK at Vong London with Jean-Georges Vongerichten. He teamed up with Nobu Matsuhisa to open Nobu London in 1997, which won a Michelin star the next year. He is now executive chef for all Nobu restaurants.

Nobu lobster salad with spicy lemon dressing

serves 4

1 x 350g live or cooked lobster (approx.)
8 whole shiitake mushrooms washed and drained mixed salad leaves of your choice
2 tsp toasted sesame seeds

for the spicy lemon dressing:

100ml freshly squeezed lemon juice
50ml soy sauce
1 large tsp finely chopped garlic
½ tsp chilli garlic sauce (you can buy this in Asian supermarkets)
1 tsp sea salt
½ tsp freshly ground black pepper
140ml grapeseed oil (available in wholefood shops)

To make the dressing, mix all the ingredients together except the oil. Mix well to dissolve the salt, then add the oil. (This can be done well in advance and will keep for up to a month in the refrigerator.)

If the lobster is live, bring a saucepan of salted water to the boil (large enough to cover the lobster). Plunge the lobster head first into the water, bring back to the boil and simmer for 6 minutes. Remove the lobster and plunge into a bowl of iced water to cool. Remove the tail and claws from the body and crack the shell. Remove the meat (discarding the pale stomach sac, the gills and the dark digestive tract), cut into bite-sized slices and reserve.

Clean and wipe the shiitake mushrooms and cut off the stems with a pair of scissors. Then either place under the grill or dry-fry in a frying pan until cooked, around 5 minutes in a pan or up to 10 under the grill.

For the salad you can use any type of leaves, but peppery ones such as rocket or mizuna work particularly well. Place the washed, drained leaves into a bowl and add a small amount of dressing. Sprinkle with some of the sesame seeds and mix gently. Place the salad in the centre of a serving dish and spoon the remaining dressing around the edge, placing the lobster pieces on top. Garnish with more sesame seeds and the cooked shiitake mushrooms.

Mourad Mazouz

Mourad Mazouz is a highly successful restaurateur. He is behind the very glamorous Sketch, which houses restaurants, bars and a gallery, and North African restaurant Momo, both in London, as well as several venues in Paris, including Derrière. He was born in Algeria and considers himself a nomad, having lived and worked all over the world, from America to Indonesia.

Scallops, mozzarella di buffala and spicy strawberry juice

serves 4 as a starter
250g fresh strawberries
freshly ground black pepper
2 limes, juice and zest
2 mozzarella di buffala
100ml good-quality olive oil
sea salt
8 grissini breadsticks
1 romaine lettuce
120g extra-large fresh scallops (clean and out of the shell)
30g butter
10ml honey

For the spicy strawberry juice, clean the strawberries, quarter them, and add a pinch of the black pepper, and 1 lime's juice and zest. Put in an ovenproof bowl, cover the mix with cling film and cook it slowly in a bain marie (or use a roasting tin half-filled with just simmering water) for 1 hour in a low oven. Strain the mix and then put the clear juice in the fridge to cool. Just before serving, put it into 4 shot glasses with some crushed ice.

Cut each mozzarella in two and season them with a good olive oil, sea salt and black pepper. Arrange on a plate with the grissini. Wash the lettuce. Cut it into strips and reserve. Season the scallops with fine salt on both sides. Heat some olive oil in a non-stick frying pan. Throw in the scallops for 40 seconds on one side and then 20 seconds on the other.

Take the pan off the heat and add the butter. Deglaze the scallops with the rest of the lime juice and season with pepper, lime zest and sea salt. Turn them over and glaze the other side of the scallops with honey. Leaving the juices in the pan, put the scallops on the plate with the grissini. Add the salad leaves to the scallop pan briefly to warm and coat with the juices, then put them into a bowl. Serve with the strawberry juice, mozzarella, grissini and scallops.

4 good things to do with Brie

Brie tart
Take a sheet of good-quality ready-rolled puff pastry and brush all over with beaten egg. Cut enough ½ cm-thick slices of Brie (you can also use Camembert) to cover most of the pastry. Lay them on the pastry, leaving about 2cm free around the edge. Scatter over some thyme leaves or sprigs and bake in a medium oven until the pastry is puffed up and golden. Serve in thin slices with a sweet chutney.

Whole baked cheese
There are two ways to do this: you can either bake the cheese in its box, or wrap it in puff pastry (see right). If you bake it in its box, just remove the paper from the cheese, put it back in the box and bake for 20 minutes or so, at 200°C/ gas 6. Carefully cut the top rind off, revealing the hot melted cheese beneath. This is good for parties, as people can dip bread or even sturdy potato crisps in it. It's tasty with something both sweet and sharp, like cranberry jelly.

Whole baked cheese in pastry
Cut two circles out of some ready-rolled puff pastry, 5cm larger than the cheese. Put the cheese in the middle of one and place the other on top. Seal the two circles well and brush with beaten egg – cut two holes in the top for the steam. Bake in a hot oven until the pastry is puffed up and golden. When you serve, be careful, as the hot cheese may gush out when you slice it.

Brie and potatoes
Adapt Eric Chavot's recipe on page 275 by omitting the bacon and instead using slices of ripe Brie (too firm and it won't melt into the pie). Or simply layer slices of parboiled waxy potatoes with Brie and cooked sliced onions, finishing with a layer of Brie, then cover with half milk, half cream, which you've infused with onion and a bay leaf for a few minutes. Season and bake until the cheese is browned and the potato cooked through – about 40 minutes at 180°C/gas 4.

Tom Norrington-Davies

Tom Norrington-Davies is a cook and a writer. He is the author of *Just Like Mother Used to Make*, *Cupboard Love* and *Game*, which he co-wrote with his friend and colleague Trish Hilferty. He is head chef and co-owner of Great Queen Street restaurant in London. He regularly writes about food in the national press and frequently for *Observer Food Monthly*.

Roast quail with puy lentils

serves 2
4 small or 2 large quail
1 tin or vac-pack of cooked puy lentils
2 large or 3 small shallots
3 tomatoes
vinaigrette of your choice
3–4 handfuls of fresh parsley

Roast 1 or 2 quails per person at 220°C/gas 7 for about 20 minutes. While they cook, drain the cooked puy lentils. Dice the shallots as finely as possible. Deseed and chop the tomatoes and mix them with the shallots and lentils. Dress with your favourite vinaigrette and lots of chopped parsley. Serve the quails on top of the lentils.

My SECRET ingredient

I think these days it is pickled walnuts. I use them for an alarming amount of things. They are great with just about any grilled fish, but particularly skate, pollack or whiting. There is no better relish for a burger. If you don't believe me, try it. Or chop up a pickled walnut and fold it with parsley, capers, mustard and a little oil: the best parsley sauce ever.

Martin Nisbet

Warm salad of pork belly with beetroot, kohlrabi and apple

serves 4
olive oil
500g raw pork belly off the bone
salt and pepper
1 onion
1 carrot
½ a leek
1 stick of celery
2 cloves of garlic
1 sprig of thyme
50g tomato purée
½ a bottle of red wine
500ml chicken stock

to serve:
4 large beetroot
2 Cox's apples
2 kohlrabi

for the dressing:
1 lemon
80ml olive oil
100g fresh soft herbs (parsley, tarragon, chives, chervil)

Heat a frying pan with a little oil. Season the pork belly on both sides with salt and pepper and cook in the hot oil until golden brown on both sides. Remove from the pan and place in a deep roasting tray.

Roughly chop the vegetables and garlic and add to the pan in which you have just fried the pork, allowing the vegetables to caramelise slightly. Add the thyme and tomato purée and continue to cook for a further 2–3 minutes. Once the tomato purée has darkened slightly, add the red wine and reduce by three-quarters.

Once the wine has reduced, add the chicken stock and bring to the boil. Strain the stock over the pork belly and cover with aluminium foil. Place in a preheated oven at 120°C/gas ½ for 3 hours. Test the belly after 3 hours by pushing a spoon through the meat. If it goes through with no resistance then it is cooked, if not then continue to cook until you feel no resistance. Once the belly is cooked, remove from the roasting tray and press between two clean trays. Place in the fridge with a weight on top and chill overnight. The following day remove the pork belly from the fridge and cut into 4 equal-sized pieces. Cut each piece into 5 slices and reserve until ready to serve.

Meanwhile wrap the beetroot in aluminium foil with a little salt, pepper and olive oil. Place in the oven at 180°C/gas 4 for 1 hour. Allow the beetroot to cool slightly, then remove the foil and peel them. Cut into ½ cm slices and (using a 2cm cutter if you have one) cut a disc from each slice. Place all the beetroot trimmings in a liquidiser and blend with a little water to make a purée.

To prepare the apple and kohlrabi, using a small melon baller (a solfrino scoop), scoop out small balls from the apple and kohlrabi. Blanch the kohlrabi in salted boiling water for 2 minutes, then refresh in iced water.

To make the dressing, juice the lemon and mix with the olive oil and season with salt and pepper. Mix the apple and kohlrabi with the lemon dressing. Take half the herbs and finely chop them, then mix with the apple and kohlrabi.

To serve, pan-fry the pork slices till golden brown. Drain on kitchen paper and season with sea salt. Spoon some beetroot purée around 4 plates. Arrange the beetroot discs, apple and kohlrabi around the plate and drizzle some dressing over and around them. Place the pork belly on the beetroot. Take the remaining herbs and dress with a little of the lemon dressing, then scatter over the warm pork.

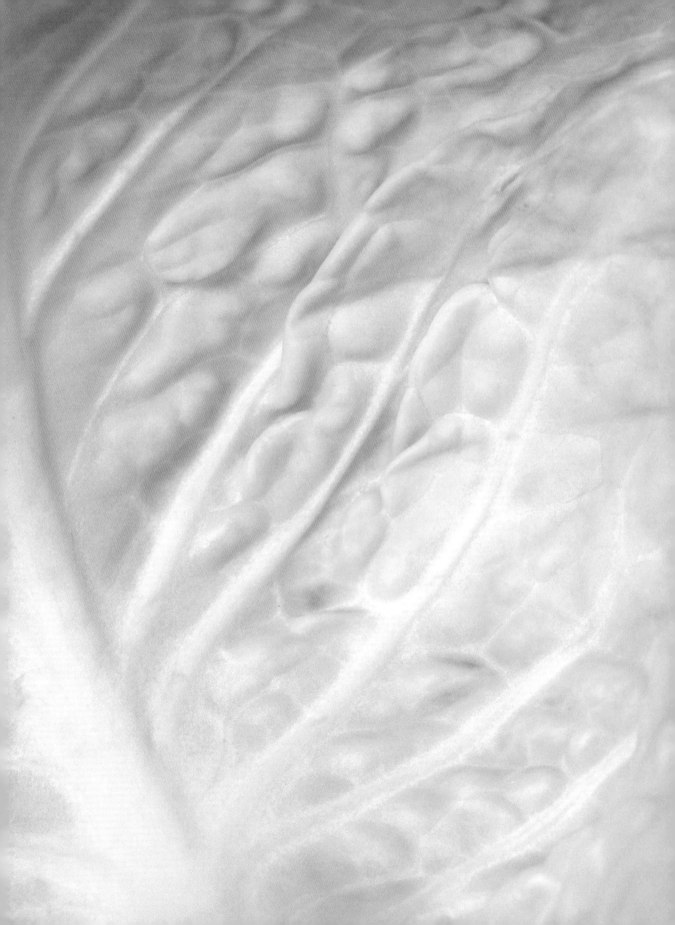

4 good things to do with cabbage

Cavolo nero and sausages

Make a simple tomato sauce with some onions, garlic and a little basil. Get some good garlicky Italian sausages, slice them into 2cm pieces and brown them thoroughly in a pan. Mix them with the tomato sauce. Layer the tomato sauce with layers of grated hard cheese or cheese sauce, or mozzarella, and layers of blanched whole leaves of cavolo nero (though you could use savoy or similar) as if they're sheets of lasagne. Finish with a layer of tomato, then cheese or cheese sauce. Grate over some Parmesan, then cook in a hot oven until the top is browned and bubbling

Garlic and black pepper cabbage

An easy way to jazz up cabbage as a side: slice a head of green cabbage or kale into ribbons. Melt a little butter in a big saucepan, then add the cabbage and allow to sizzle for 30 seconds. Add a ladleful or two of hot stock (vegetable or chicken) and clamp a lid down on the cabbage. Allow to steam for a few minutes until tender, stirring occasionally to prevent sticking. Finally, take the lid off, turn up the heat to briefly boil down the remaining stock, and thoroughly stir in ½ a clove of crushed garlic. Grind over lots of black pepper and serve.

Coleslaw

There are many options for this – just choose your favourite ingredients. Shred a mixture of raw red and white cabbage, with the addition of any of the following: carrots, celeriac, turnips, radishes, beetroot or fennel, also shredded. Add finely sliced onions or shallots and make a dressing with yoghurt or mayonnaise and a handful of chopped, fresh, soft green herbs – parsley, chervil, dill or even mint, plus a little lemon juice and some olive oil to loosen it. Season to taste.

Cabbage with pancetta

Fry pancetta lardons gently until crisp. In another pan, steam strips of cabbage that have been washed with the water still clinging to the leaves for a couple of minutes until tender. When done, stir in a knob of butter and the pancetta. Eat while hot.

TRICKS OF THE TRADE

'Put green vegetables in water with a bit of ascorbic acid
(vitamin C or lemon juice) to keep them bright green
while you are making your recipe.'

Alain Ducasse

Stuart Gillies

Stuart Gillies is head chef at the Boxwood Café, part of the Gordon Ramsay group of restaurants, having previously worked with Angela Hartnett at the Connaught in London and for the legendary Daniel Boulud at Daniel's in New York. He is executive chef of Gordon Ramsay Plane Food at Heathrow Terminal Five and is overseeing the reopening of the Savoy Grill. He regularly appears on *GMTV*, *Saturday Kitchen* and *The Great British Menu*.

Apple tatin

serves 4
5 Braeburn apples
200g caster sugar
50g butter
400g puff pastry (shop-bought is fine)

Peel and cut the apples into quarters, removing the core. Leave them in the fridge overnight to dry out. Place the sugar into a large pan on a medium heat. As the sugar starts to caramelise, continue heating until it becomes a dark, rich colour. Place the apples in the caramel and roast for 2–3 minutes. Then add the butter to the apples and cook for a further 4–5 minutes. The apples should be almost cooked without breaking down. Carefully, put the apples on a tray and cool in the fridge. Save all the extra caramel.

Place the apples in 4 small individual ovenproof frying pans (or you can use one big pan) with a cut side facing down. Place 4 pieces in the bottom of each pan, with 1 piece in the middle (or arrange all of them in a single layer if you're using one big pan). Roll the puff pastry thin, then use a plate or saucer to cut out a circle a little larger than your pan and place over the apples. Drizzle some of the extra caramel around the edge of the pastry (you may need to melt it again) and tuck the pastry into the pan and around the apples. Bake in the oven at 180°C/gas 4 for 15–16 minutes. The pastry should be crisp. Once it is ready, tip out upside-down very carefully onto a plate so you can see the presentation side, and drizzle with extra caramel if you like.

I buy wild **West Mersea oysters** from Wright Bros in Borough Market, London. I particularly like the wild West Mersea oyster as it's very robust and can be served natural or cooked. It's also a British variety, and sourced traditionally by a seventh-generation oyster fisherman, Richard Howard.

Oliver Peyton

Pimm's lollipops

A quintessentially British treat packed full of refreshing fruit and with the added kick of Pimm's. We make these whenever we have friends over – they are real icebreakers in the truest sense. Keep these out of reach of the kids!

makes 8
280ml Pimm's No 1
800ml organic lemonade
2 leaves of mint, finely chopped
80g Cox's apples, cut into small dice
80g William pears, cut into small dice
80g cucumber, cut into small dice

Mix together all the ingredients. Pour into the lollipop moulds and place in the freezer. As the mixture begins to freeze, give it an occasional stir so that the fruit becomes suspended in the ice.

Recently, I've been using a lot of verjuice, which is made by pressing unripe grapes. It would have been made traditionally in the UK with crab apples. I use it to add sharpness to sauces, salads and fish where a lemon or vinegar flavour would overpower anything delicate.

Shaun Hill

Buttermilk pudding with baked cardamom figs

serves 6
for the buttermilk pudding:
200ml double cream
250g caster sugar
1 vanilla pod, split
4 strips of orange peel
juice of ½ a lemon
3 leaves of gelatine – soaked in cold water
600ml buttermilk
200ml whipped cream

for the baked figs:
9 figs
1 tsp crushed cardamom seeds
1 tbs caster sugar
juice of 1 orange
1 tbs clear honey

Bring the double cream, sugar, vanilla and orange peel to the boil. Remove from the heat, then add the lemon juice and softened gelatine. Strain into a clean jug. Put the buttermilk in a bowl, then gradually whisk in the hot cream. Cool the mixture, then fold in the whipped cream. Spoon the mix into dariole moulds or ramekins and refrigerate overnight.

Halve the figs. Arrange in a baking dish, then sprinkle over the cardamom, sugar, orange juice and honey. Bake until hot, then remove from the oven. Place 3 fig halves at the side of each pudding with a little of the cooking liquor.

October

Cauliflowers are at their peak, and apples, including the first Bramleys, beetroots, broccoli, carrots, figs, Jerusalem artichokes, leeks, marrows, mushrooms, onions, pears, plums, maincrop potatoes, sprouts and squash are all good this month.

Treat yourself to Joël Robuchon's incredibly rich mashed potato, Fergus Henderson's famous parsley and roast bone marrow salad, or make the most of the season's apples with Tom Kitchin's wonderful apple pie.

Mark Hix

Cauliflower cheese

This is one of my all-time favourite dishes.

serves 4–6
1 medium cauliflower
1l milk
½ a bay leaf
salt and freshly ground black pepper
60g butter
60g plain flour
100ml double cream
120g mature cheddar cheese, grated
1–2 tbs finely chopped parsley

Cut the cauliflower into florets, reserving the leaves and stalk. Bring the milk to the boil in a saucepan, with the bay leaf added, and season well with salt and pepper. Add the cauliflower florets and leaves and simmer for about 7–8 minutes until tender. Drain in a colander over a bowl to reserve the milk.

Melt the butter in a heavy-based pan and stir in the flour. Continue stirring over a low heat for about 30 seconds, then gradually stir in the reserved hot milk, using a whisk. Bring to a simmer and turn the heat down very low (use a heat diffuser if you have one). Continue to simmer very gently for 20 minutes, stirring every so often to ensure that the sauce doesn't catch on the bottom.

Add the cream and simmer for a couple of minutes. The sauce should be of a thick coating consistency by now; if not, simmer for a little longer. Strain through a fine sieve into a bowl, whisk in three-quarters of the cheese, then taste and adjust the seasoning if necessary.

Preheat the oven to 220°C/gas 7 (or the grill to medium-high). Make sure the cauliflower is dry – you can use kitchen paper to pat dry if necessary. Mix the cauliflower with half of the cheese sauce and transfer to an ovenproof dish. Spoon the rest of the sauce over and scatter the chopped parsley and the rest of the cheese on top. Either bake in the oven for about 20 minutes until golden, or reheat and brown under the grill.

Joël Robuchon

French chef Joël Robuchon was named Chef of the Century by the guide *Gault Millau* in 1989, and went on to surpass even that achievement by winning twenty-five Michelin stars. He has restaurants in Taipei, Hong Kong, Las Vegas, Macau, Monaco, New York, Paris, Tokyo and London. He has published several books and chaired the committee for *Larousse Gastronomique*. This is one of his most famous dishes.

Purée de pommes de terre (mashed potato)

serves 6
1kg potatoes, preferably rates or BF15, scrubbed but unpeeled
coarse salt
250g butter, diced and kept well chilled until use
250ml whole milk
salt and pepper

Put the potatoes in a saucepan with 2 litres of cold water and 1 tbs coarse salt. Bring to a simmer, cover, and cook until a knife slips in the potatoes easily and cleanly, about 25 minutes.

Drain the potatoes and peel them. Put them through a potato ricer (or a food mill fitted with its finest disc) into a large saucepan. Turn the heat to medium and dry the potato flesh out a bit by turning it vigorously with a spatula for about 5 minutes.

Meanwhile, rinse a small saucepan and pour out the excess water but don't wipe it dry. Add the milk and bring to a boil.

Turn the heat under the potatoes to low and incorporate the well-chilled butter bit by bit, stirring it in energetically for a smooth, creamy finish. Pour in the very hot milk in a thin stream, still over a low heat, still stirring briskly. Keep stirring until all the milk is absorbed. Turn off the heat and taste for salt and pepper. For an even lighter, finer purée, put it through a very fine sieve before serving.

Richard Bertinet

Richard Bertinet is a chef and baker originally from Brittany. He now lives in Bath, where he runs the Bertinet Kitchen, his acclaimed cookery school. Prior to opening the school in 2005, he worked at the Chewton Glen Hotel and the Rhinefield House Hotel in the New Forest, and the Silver Plough at Pitton in Salisbury. His third book, *Cook*, is out now.

Oxtail au vin rouge

serves 4–6
1.2kg large oxtails
30g lard
2 bottles of red burgundy
1 pork rind, about 150g
4 cloves of garlic, unpeeled and crushed
8 shallots, peeled and left whole
1 onion, thinly sliced
1 bouquet garni
400g carrots, peeled and cut into 1cm rounds
300ml beef or veal stock
6 peppercorns, crushed
200g field mushrooms, if possible, or button mushrooms
½ a celeriac
1 tbs flat-leaved parsley leaves
salt and freshly ground pepper

Soak the oxtails in cold water for several hours. Cut off any excess fat, then cut the tails into pieces through the joints and pat dry on a tea towel.

Preheat the oven to 160°C/gas 2–3.

In a large flameproof casserole, heat the lard, put in the pieces of oxtail and seal for about 6 minutes until well browned on all sides. Bring the red wine to the boil in a saucepan.

Remove the oxtail from the casserole and line the bottom of the casserole with the pork rind, laying it flat side down. Return the oxtail to the casserole, then add the garlic, whole shallots, onion, bouquet garni and carrots. Pour in the wine and stock, salt slightly, add the crushed peppercorns and bring to the boil. Cover the oxtail with greaseproof paper, then with the lid of the pan, and cook in the preheated oven for 2 hours.

Wipe the mushrooms clean and trim off the stalks if necessary. Peel the celeriac and cut into quarters or into 6 pieces depending on size. Place in a saucepan, cover with cold water, bring to the boil, blanch, refresh and drain. When the oxtail has been cooking for 2 hours, add the mushrooms and the celeriac and cook for another hour.

Carefully lift the oxtail and vegetables from the casserole, using a slotted spoon. Immediately reduce the sauce until it lightly coats the back of a spoon, then discard the pork rind and bouquet garni. Scatter the oxtail and vegetables into a deep serving dish. Skim off the fat from the surface of the sauce if necessary, season with salt and pepper to taste and pour the boiling sauce over the oxtail and vegetables. Sprinkle with parsley.

My essential ingredient is a jar of **Dijon mustard**. I use it in my dressings and in fresh mayonnaise, I love it with charcuterie and I could not eat Sunday lunch without it.

Shaun Hill
Herbed white fish with sourdough

Paint a slice of white fish (sole is nice, but then so is gurnard) with olive oil, then grill, along with some similarly treated sourdough bread. Blend some parsley, and maybe whatever other herbs strike your fancy, along with a shot of white wine, a crushed clove of garlic, some olive oil and salt and pepper so that you have a thickish sauce-cum-dressing. Spoon this over the grilled bread, fish and some salad leaves. Bob's your uncle.

Mitch Tonks
Speedy spiced tagine

I like spicy food and always keep packs of spice from www.sambavaspices.com, which is run by my friend James. His tagine mix is the best, so if you get some, try this: gently sweat some finely chopped onions, ginger and garlic in a little olive oil, add a couple of spoonfuls of the spice mix, some chunks of gurnard, monkfish and mussels, simmer gently for 20 minutes, season with salt and pepper, then add a good squeeze of lemon and some finely chopped coriander for a really quick seafood tagine.

Anna Hansen
Skate with clams and chorizo

Pan-fry a piece of skate with some diced chorizo, a handful of clams, a handful of halved cherry tomatoes and a pinch of saffron. Slosh over a decent slug of white wine and cover with a lid until the fish is cooked and the clams have opened. Serve with roast sweet potatoes, endive and a generous sprinkling of parsley.

Raymond Blanc
Smoked salmon omelette

In a mixing bowl, gently beat 3 medium, organic/free-range, fresh eggs together (but don't break them down too much) with a pinch of salt and pepper. In an omelette pan, heat a tsp olive oil and another of butter until it begins to foam. Pour in the egg and cook for a few seconds, allowing the omelette to set lightly before stirring the set part inwards. Repeat this motion 5 times. Put 30g or 2 tbs roughly chopped smoked salmon in the middle of the omelette and fold the sides towards the centre, then turn out onto a plate. Brush with olive oil or butter and serve.

Claude Bosi

Claude Bosi is chef-patron of Hibiscus, a Michelin-starred restaurant he runs with his wife, Claire. Born in Lyons, he has worked in great restaurants like Raymond Point Carré and Michael Rostang in Paris, and La Pyramide in Vienna. He originally opened Hibiscus in Shropshire in 2000, and moved it to London in 2007.

Scallop carpaccio with black radish and truffle

serves 4
8 large scallops, cleaned and roe removed
almond oil
1 black radish, sliced thinly
1 lemon
chopped parsley, thyme and tarragon
2 tbs truffle dressing
fresh black truffle

for the truffle dressing:
100ml truffle juice
1 tsp sherry vinegar
150ml grapeseed oil

Slice each scallop into 8–10 slices. Put a few drops of almond oil on the base of a plate and glaze it using a brush to coat (this makes arranging the scallops and radish less tricky!).

Make the truffle dressing. Reduce the truffle juice on a low heat, then add the sherry vinegar. Gently whisk in the oil. You can buy truffle juice online – its intensity can vary, so be guided by your own taste.

Arrange the scallop and radish slices by overlapping them on the plate: 2 slices of scallop, 1 slice of radish; 2 slices of scallop, 1 slice of radish – following the shape of the plate – until all the pieces have been used. Grate lemon zest over them and sprinkle over the herbs. Dot the truffle dressing around the plate. Serve with grated fresh truffle.

I use Baldechre strong unbleached white organic flour – I am very fussy about my puff pastry and this flour is perfect for making it. It's made in the old-fashioned way and tastes so light in the pastry. When it's sent to us it's so fresh, the paper bag is still warm.

Mitch Tonks

Scallops as cooked at the Seahorse

serves 2
100g butter
2 cloves of garlic
a handful of parsley leaves
2 salted anchovy fillets
a splash of Tabasco
6 scallops and their shells
1 tsp tarragon, finely chopped
6 tbs white wine
6 tbs olive oil
sea salt
6 tbs fine breadcrumbs

Preheat your oven to maximum. First, make the garlic butter by placing the butter, garlic, parsley and anchovy fillets in a food processor with a splash of Tabasco. Blitz until you have a smooth green butter.

Place a scallop in each shell, keeping the roe on. Sprinkle each one with a little tarragon, then add 1 tbs wine to each scallop and 1 tbs olive oil. Season with a little salt. Then place 1 tsp garlic butter on the top of each scallop, and sprinkle breadcrumbs over each one.

Place your scallops on a roasting dish and cook in a hot oven for 5 minutes. The breadcrumbs should be nicely browned, the scallops firmed up and the olive oil, butter, garlic and wine all bubbling together. Serve 3 scallops to a plate, or one plate of 6 to share, and get stuck in.

(This recipe is taken from *Fish.*)

Chris Galvin

With his brother Jeff, Chris Galvin runs Galvin Bistrot de Luxe, Michelin-starred Galvin at Windows and the newly opened Galvin La Chapelle and Café de Luxe in London. He has been working as a chef for thirty years on both sides of the Atlantic, and before setting up these restaurants he worked at the Wolseley and for Sir Terence Conran.

Creamy spiced mussel soup

serves 2
500g mussels
1 glass of dry white wine
1 glass of fish stock
butter
2 shallots, chopped
garlic, to taste
a pinch (or more) of curry powder
a pinch of saffron
a splash of whipping cream
salt and pepper
parsley, chopped

Cook the mussels in the fish stock and wine for a couple of minutes, then drain, reserving the stock (discard any that have not opened). Heat some butter in a pan and add the shallots, garlic and curry powder. Add a pinch of saffron and stir in the warm stock, bring it to the boil and then add a generous splash of whipping cream. Reduce the soup by a third and season with salt and pepper. Serve in soup bowls and garnish with parsley for a light and flavoursome soup.

I like **Sel de Guérande** because it brings life to so many ingredients. Crumbled on a piece of roast beef it is like icing on a cake.

4 good things to do with steak

Steak with shallot sauce

Cook a good steak until it's done to your liking. Allow it to rest and keep it warm. In the meantime (preferably in the same pan) soften and brown some halved or quartered shallots (or onions, sliced into chunks) in butter, then when they're soft and just beginning to catch, splash over 1/2 a glass of red wine and the same of stock (preferably beef). Bubble off the alcohol and allow to reduce. Add a little flour to thicken it if you like. Taste and season with salt and pepper. Pour this hearty sauce over the steak.

Béarnaise sauce

Reduce 100ml white wine vinegar, 2 finely chopped shallots and 1/2 a finely chopped clove of garlic over a low heat for about half an hour. Strain, cool, and mix with 3 egg yolks, then immediately place the mixture in a heatproof bowl over just simmering water, stirring constantly. Add around 150g butter in little chunks, and finally mix in a finely chopped sprig of tarragon.

Green peppercorn sauce

In a frying pan (perhaps the one you just cooked your steak in) foam a couple of knobs of butter. Add a couple of tsp green peppercorns in brine. Stir in a crushed clove of garlic and 1 tbs cognac, then whisk in a dollop of smooth Dijon mustard, and about 100ml whipping cream. Simmer very gently until saucy.

Caper sauce

In the hot pan you cooked your steak in, pour 1/2 a glass of white wine and deglaze the crunchy bits. Boil off the alcohol then add a knob of butter and 4–5 tbs whipping cream. Simmer gently to reduce. Whisk in 1 tbs Dijon mustard and finally stir in a couple of tsp capers (rinsed), some chopped fresh parsley and some black pepper.

TRICKS OF THE TRADE

'Add soy sauce to gravy to get great colour and flavour.'

Tim Hughes

Fergus Henderson

Fergus Henderson co-founded St John Restaurant near London's Smithfield meat market in 1994, and the restaurant's nose-to-tail offal-eating ethos was immediately popular with diners and influenced many other chefs and menus. He opened another restaurant, St John Bread and Wine, in Spitalfields in 2003, and a St John Hotel will open in 2010 in Chinatown. He has written two books: *Nose to Tail Eating* and *Beyond Nose to Tail Eating*.

Roast bone marrow and parsley salad

This is one dish that is always on the menu at St John. The marrowbone comes from a calf's leg – ask your butcher to keep some for you. You will need teaspoons or long, thin implements to scrape your marrow out of the bone.

serves 4
12 x 7–8cm pieces of middle veal marrowbone
1 healthy bunch of parsley, picked from its stems
2 shallots, peeled and thinly sliced
a modest handful of capers, extra-fine if possible
a pinch of sea salt and pepper
a good supply of toast
coarse sea salt

for the dressing:
juice of 1 lemon
extra-virgin olive oil

Put the marrowbone in an ovenproof frying pan and place in a hot oven. The roasting process should take about 20 minutes, depending on the thickness of the bone. You are looking for the marrow to be loose and giving, but not to have melted away, which it will do if left too long (traditionally the ends would be covered to prevent any seepage, but I like the colouring and crispiness that they take on).

Meanwhile, lightly chop your parsley, just enough to discipline it, mix it with the shallots and capers, and, at the last moment, dress.

This is a dish that should not be completely seasoned before leaving the kitchen, rendering a last-minute seasoning necessary by the actual eater – this, especially in the case of coarse sea salt, gives texture and uplift at the moment of eating. My approach is to scrape the marrow from the bone onto the toast and season with coarse sea salt. Then put a pinch of parsley salad on top of this and eat.

Tom Oldroyd

Chickpea, leek and fennel soup

serves 4 as a main, 6 as a starter
500g dried chickpeas
chicken stock
a pinch of dried chilli
1 finely diced shallot
2 leeks cut into 1cm pieces
2 small fennel cut into 1cm pieces
salt and pepper
good olive oil

Cover the chickpeas in water and soak overnight. Drain and cover with chicken stock – there should be enough stock so that it covers the chickpeas by 3 or 4cm. Add a pinch of dried chilli, and cook until tender. If you don't have enough time to soak the chickpeas, you can use tinned ones instead.

In a large pan, sweat the shallot, leeks and fennel in a little olive oil until soft. Season with salt and pepper.

Combine the chickpeas, including the stock, and the vegetables and simmer for 5 minutes. Remove a quarter of the vegetables and chickpeas and set to one side. Blend the remainder of the chickpea and vegetable mixture until smooth. Add the whole chickpeas and vegetables back to the soup and season to taste. Serve with a dash of good olive oil.

4 good things to do with apples

Apple and sultana cake

Swap the bananas and Twix in Eric Chavot's cake on page 70 for lightly caramelised chunks of 2 cored and peeled eating apples, and a handful of sultanas (which you could soak in liqueur if you fancy, first).

Pork and apple burgers

Grate a smallish cooking apple very finely and mix with 800g minced pork, a beaten egg and 1 tbs shredded sage. Season with salt and pepper, shape into burgers and cook on a medium heat for 7 or 8 minutes each side, until browned and cooked all the way through. Serve on a bun with some raw or cooked onions.

Cider and apple relish for meat

To go with roast pork: put 4 cooking apples, peeled, cored and chopped, into a pan with 250ml dry cider. Allow to cook down until the fruit is pulpy and the alcohol has burned off. Grate over a little nutmeg and, if you like spice, add a whole chilli which you've slit down one side. Taste and add some sugar if it's too sharp. Reduce on a low simmer until it's the texture of apple sauce. Remove the chilli before serving.

Apple salad

Very thinly slice a cored sharp eating apple and add to a salad of warm halloumi which you've sliced, floured and fried until golden, with a dressing of lime juice and olive oil. Toss with your preferred salad leaves.

Tom Kitchin

Tom Kitchin began his career at the Gleneagles Hotel near his childhood home outside Kinross and has worked with Pierre Koffmann, Guy Savoy and Alain Ducasse. He and his wife Michaela opened The Kitchin on Edinburgh's Leith waterfront in 2006 – it won a Michelin star six months later, when he was just twenty-nine. His book is called *From Nature to Plate: A Seasonal Journey*.

Apple pie
This is one of my favourite autumn puddings.

serves 6
2 large cooking apples, peeled and cored
100g sugar
2 tbs flour
1 tsp cinnamon
2 large Granny Smith apples, peeled and cored

1 egg, beaten

for the sweet pastry:
500g flour
100g icing sugar
350g unsalted butter
1 egg, beaten

Chop the cooking apples and put them in a pan with the sugar and flour (adding flour helps to retain juices and so stops the crust getting soggy). Add 75ml water and cook over a low heat until the apple is soft, then add the cinnamon and mix with a wooden spoon to make a smooth purée. Slice the Granny Smiths and fold into the purée.

To make the pastry, sift the flour and sugar together. Pulse them with the butter in a food processor until the mix resembles breadcrumbs. Mix in the egg until the dough clings together, then knead gently. Flatten the dough into a round, and divide into 2 pieces. Wrap each in cling film and chill in the fridge for 15 minutes.

Preheat the oven to 230°C/gas 8 and grease a 23cm pie dish. Roll out one piece of dough into a circle about 10cm bigger than your pie dish. Use this to line the dish, then spoon in the apple mixture. Roll out the second piece of dough to the same size and lay it carefully over the pie. Tuck the edges of the top crust under the lower crust and press them together. Cut a few vents in the top crust with a sharp knife and brush the pastry with the egg. Place the pie on the lowest rack of the preheated oven and bake for 10 minutes. Lower the temperature to 180°C/gas 4 and bake for another 25–30 minutes. To serve, dust with some icing sugar and serve with whipped cream or vanilla ice cream.

Moutarde de Meaux Pommery is a good-quality pommery mustard that can be used with anything from beef or rabbit to delicate shellfish such as clams or razorfish.

November

Apples, cabbage, carrots, cauliflower, leeks, parsnips, pears, potatoes, pumpkin, quinces, sprouts, squash and swede are all good this month.

This month, take the time to make Raymond Blanc's fabulous coq au vin, Sam and Sam Clark's jewelled pumpkin rice, or Jay Rayner's easy chorizo stew. For pudding, try Tristan Welch's rich Cambridge burnt cream.

Ruth Rogers and Rose Gray

Ruth Rogers and Rose Gray opened the River Café in 1987, and it rapidly became one of the most important and influential restaurants in the UK, with a stream of brilliant chefs emerging from its kitchens. The Italian menu changes twice daily and is inspired by Ruth and Rose's passion for Italy, and their experiences of living and cooking there. They wrote many wonderful books together, including their latest, *The River Café Classic Italian Cookbook*, which includes this recipe. Rose Gray sadly passed away in early 2010.

Zuppe alle vongole (clam soup)

Every Friday the fish sellers from Grosseto bring fish to the hill town of Montalcino. They sell from what is literally a hole in the walls of the town, but step inside and there is an abundance of glistening fresh fish – different sizes of squid, sea bass, swordfish, anchovies, clams and mussels. You have to get there early – and even then there is a queue – for by ten o'clock it is all gone. We bought clams and cooked them this way; the toast absorbs the delicious broth.

serves 6
2kg small clams, washed
extra-virgin olive oil
3 cloves of garlic, peeled and finely chopped
2 dried red chillies, crumbled
3 tbs chopped fresh flat-leaf parsley
1 bottle of dry white wine, such as Vermentino
12 small slices of sourdough bread

Check over the clams and discard any that are not closed. Heat 2 tbs olive oil in a thick-bottomed saucepan large enough to hold the clams. Add all the garlic and chillies and half the parsley and cook for a few minutes. Add the wine, bring to the boil, cook for a minute, then add the clams. Stir well, to coat the clams with the wine. Cover the saucepan and cook the clams over a fairly high heat until they open, which will take 2 or 3 minutes. Discard any that remain closed.

Toast or grill the bread until brown, then prop up the pieces around the sides of a warmed oval dish. With a slotted spoon, remove the clams to the dish. Reduce the wine in the saucepan for a few minutes more, then pour over the clams. Sprinkle over the remaining parsley and drizzle with plenty of extra-virgin olive oil.

Natoora smoked pancetta is an absolute essential in the fridge. It's basically a bacon substitute, but a superb one.

Raymond Blanc

Raymond Blanc, who is from the Comté region in France, is a totally self-taught chef. His hotel, Le Manoir aux Quat' Saisons in Oxfordshire, where he also has a cookery school, has had two Michelin stars for twenty-five years. He is often on TV, and his most recent series, *Kitchen Secrets*, was a great success. His latest book is *A Taste of My Life*.

Coq au vin

serves 4
for marinating the chicken:
1l full-bodied red wine
1.5kg chicken, free-range and organic, cut into 12 – including the backbone
1 medium carrot, peeled and sliced into 1.5cm pieces
½ a celery stick, sliced into 1cm pieces
1 medium onion, white, peeled and cut into 8 segments, with the root on
1 tsp whole black peppercorns
1 bouquet garni (parsley stalks, 4 bay leaves, 6 sprigs of thyme)

for braising the chicken:
2 tbs clarified butter for frying
2 tbs plain flour, sprinkled onto a baking tray and toasted in a preheated oven at 200°C/gas 6 for 10 minutes until pale brown in colour

to finish:
1 tbs clarified butter for frying
200g smoked, streaky bacon, rind removed, diced into 3cm x 1cm pieces
400g button mushrooms
sea salt and black pepper
1 tbs flat-leaf parsley, chopped

Boil the wine and reduce by one third. Leave to cool. Mix the chicken, carrot, celery, onion, peppercorns and bouquet garni together and leave to marinate for 12–24 hours.

Preheat the oven to 100°C/gas ¼ . Place a colander over a bowl and drain the marinade for 1 hour. Separate the chicken, vegetables and herbs, and pat dry. In a casserole dish on a high heat, colour the chicken in the clarified butter for 5–7 minutes on each side. With a slotted spoon, transfer the chicken on to a plate and put to one side. Add the vegetables to the same pan. Lower the heat to medium and cook for 5 minutes. Spoon out the fat, add the flour, stir for a few seconds and add the wine from the marinade little by little, whisking continuously to incorporate the flour. Lastly add the chicken and bouquet garni. The sauce should be smooth and coat the back of a spoon. Bring to the boil, skim, cover and cook in the preheated oven for 1 hour. Taste the sauce. Do not add any salt as you will be adding the bacon later.

Add the butter to a non-stick pan and cook the bacon for 3–4 minutes, until golden brown, add the mushrooms and cook for 2 minutes. Season with salt and pepper. Mix the bacon and mushrooms into the coq au vin and sprinkle with parsley.

Eric Chavot
Easy chicken cordon bleu

I don't want to cook two-Michelin-starred food at home for my kids after a hard day at work! I do a fantastic chicken cordon bleu at home. Get a nice chicken breast per person, and butterfly it. Next get a good-quality piece of smoked ham and some garlic Boursin and wrap the ham round the cheese in the shape of a cigar. Then tuck the cigar inside the chicken and pull the meat around it. Sear it in a pan until the chicken is golden, about 2 minutes each side, and then pop the whole thing in a hot oven until the chicken is cooked through.

John Torode
Foolproof roast duck

Make a stand for your duck out of 3 or 4 whole carrots in your roasting tray. Put the duck on top of the carrots, pour 2 cups of water into the tray, and cover tightly with foil. Cook for an hour at 200°C/gas 6, and then finish for 20 minutes without the foil to crisp up the skin. You can then use the carrot and duck stock to make a sauce to serve, if you like.

Fuchsia Dunlop
Egg-fried rice from leftovers

Heat a wok with a little groundnut oil, and add a couple of beaten eggs, swirling them around the base. When they are half cooked but still runny on top, add cold, cooked rice and stir-fry vigorously, breaking up the clumps of rice and seasoning with soy sauce, salt and pepper. Continue to stir-fry until the rice is very hot. Add a handful of finely sliced spring onion greens and stir a few times until you can smell them, then serve. Add anything you like to the basic recipe, such as blanched frozen peas, leftover roast pork or finely chopped cooked shrimps (make sure you heat these through).

Tom Norrington-Davies
Roast chicken with chips and mayonnaise

Rub free-range chicken legs with mild olive oil and a slightly over-generous amount of celery salt. Roast them hard and fast, and then serve with oven chips and mayonnaise, plus your favourite leaf mix. Eat this meal with your fingers.

Matt Tebbutt

Matt Tebbutt thought he wanted to be a pilot, but after learning to fly realised he wanted to cook. He has worked for Alastair Little, Sally Clarke and Bruce Poole. His restaurant is the much-loved Foxhunter near Abergavenny, which he runs with his wife Lisa, and he is a regular on *Market Kitchen*. He is the author of *Matt Tebbutt Cooks Country*.

Roasted pigeon with braised chicory and nettle butter

serves 2
4 pigeon breasts
a splash of port and Madeira
½ a cinnamon stick, broken roughly
1 finely diced shallot
1 bay leaf
1 orange, pared
1 clove of garlic, finely chopped
a few sprigs of thyme
2 heads of chicory
olive oil

3 tbs caster sugar
a pinch of nutmeg
a pinch of allspice
40g butter
salt, pepper and lemon juice

for the nettle butter:
200g (approx.) young nettles
200g salted butter, softened
freshly ground black pepper
a squeeze of lemon

Marinate the pigeon overnight in the port, Madeira, cinnamon, shallot, bay, orange peel, garlic and thyme. Cover and refrigerate. To make the butter, blanch the nettles in boiling water for no more than 30 seconds. Plunge into iced water, squeeze and chop finely. Mix with the butter, pepper and a little lemon juice. Taste and add salt. Roll into a log, wrap in baking paper and chill until hard.

Preheat the oven to 200°C/gas 6. Cut the chicory lengthways, season and heat cut-side down in a non-stick pan with a little olive oil until it starts to colour. This will take 5–8 minutes. Turn over and sprinkle each half with roughly equal quantities of sugar, the spices, and dot each with the butter. Cover with a cartouche (a circle of greaseproof paper) and roast in the hot oven until tender. If the pan looks like it's catching, add a little water or stock. Glaze the chicory with the buttery juices, and give them a squeeze of lemon. Keep warm.

In another pan, heat a film of oil, remove the pigeon from the marinade and pat dry. Season and start to fry, flesh-side down, for a few minutes. Turn the birds over and cook for another 2 minutes or so. Remove from the pan and allow to rest. The breasts must be served pink, otherwise they will be super tough. To serve, arrange the chicory halves on a large serving plate, spoon over any buttery juices, slice the pigeon breasts in half on the angle and, using a potato peeler, peel some thin lengths of the nettle butter over the dish and allow to melt in. The marinade could be heated to make a little pan sauce.

Sam and Sam Clark

Samuel and Samantha Clark opened the brilliant Moro in London's Clerkenwell in 1997. Their first book, *The Moro Cookbook*, was published in 2001 to wide acclaim, followed by *Casa Moro* and *Moro East*.

Moro jewelled pumpkin rice

serves 4–6

500g peeled and deseeded butternut squash (the flesh of a 750g squash), cut into 1 cm dice
1 tsp fine sea salt
2 tbs olive oil
a big pinch, about 50 strands, of saffron
100g unsalted butter
6cm piece of cinnamon stick
4 allspice berries, crushed
1 large or 2 medium onions, thinly sliced across the grain

15g dried barberries (or currants)
50g shelled unsalted pistachios
½ tsp ground cardamom
300g basmati rice, soaked in tepid, salted water, for 1 hour
450ml vegetable stock (or 450ml boiling water mixed with 2 tsp vegetable bouillon)

for the crispy onions:
1 very large Spanish onion, very evenly sliced
vegetable oil for frying

First, make the crispy onions. Heat 8–10mm depth of vegetable oil in a wide saucepan over a high heat. When it is hot but not smoking, add a 1cm layer of the shaved onions and reduce the heat to medium. Fry, stirring often, until they are an even golden colour. Drain and spread out on kitchen paper to cool, then repeat the process (you may need to top up the oil) until you have used all the onion.

Preheat the oven to 230°C/gas 8. Toss the diced butternut squash with half of the salt and the olive oil. Spread it in a single layer in a baking tray and roast for 30 minutes until tender. Mix the saffron with 3 tbs boiling water and add 25g of the butter. Set aside. Heat the remaining butter in a medium saucepan with the cinnamon and allspice until it foams, then add the onion and ½ tsp of salt. Fry over a medium heat for 10–15 minutes, stirring occasionally until the onion is soft and starting to colour. Add the barberries, pistachios and cardamom and cook for 10 minutes more. Now drain the rice and add to the pan, stirring for a minute or two to coat, then pour in the stock. Taste for seasoning, then add the roast squash. Cover with a circle of greaseproof paper and a tight-fitting lid and cook over a high heat for 5 minutes. Reduce the heat to low and simmer for a final 5 minutes. Remove the lid and paper and drizzle with the buttery saffron water. Replace the lid and leave to rest, off the heat, for 5–10 minutes. Serve with a scattering of crispy onions and some yoghurt seasoned with garlic, salt and pepper.

(This recipe is taken from *Moro East*.)

4 good things to do with sausages

Cream and basil

Take the meat from 4 sausages out of their cases and break up into small chunks, then cook in a little oil until brown and crispy. (You could also cook some sliced onion here too.) Remove and set aside. Add a splash of stock to deglaze the pan and then add a couple of tbs cream and some chilli flakes. Reduce to thicken very slowly. Put the sausages back in and heat through (gently, again). Stir through some basil. You can serve this with pasta or with crusty bread.

Bean and sausage stew

Break up some sausage meat as before, or cut the sausages into 3cm chunks, and brown in a little oil. Add a tin of tomatoes, 1 tbs mustard, a splash of red wine (if you have any), some black pepper, salt and a pinch of oregano. Let it all cook until the tomatoes have broken down and are saucy. Taste before serving – it should be sharp and mustardy. Finally, add a drained and rinsed tin of cannellini or butter beans. Stir and heat through. Serve in bowls with crusty bread.

One-pot eggs and sausages

Make a simple tomato sauce with passata, a little onion softly fried in olive oil, garlic if you like and some salt and pepper. Keep warm. Fry some sausages – chipolatas work well – in your largest frying pan until brown and cooked through. Make enough space in the middle of the pan for a couple of eggs and fry them in the sausage fat. When done to your liking, tip the tomato sauce into the pan over the eggs and sausages, then scatter with chives and/or parsley. Eat straight from the pan. A delicious brunch or supper.

Roasted squash

Peel, deseed and chop up a squash or pumpkin into walnut-sized pieces. Roast in a hot oven until browning and soft. Meanwhile, break up some sausages as before, and fry in a little oil until browned with a couple of whole cloves of garlic, peeled and slightly squashed, and some shallot or onion. Once cooked, turn the heat down and stir in some crème fraiche or cream. Reduce gently. Cook some pasta in salted water. Remove the cooked squash from the oven and add to the sausage sauce. Toss with the cooked pasta and season lightly. You might like to add a couple of shredded sage leaves as well.

TRICKS OF THE TRADE

'You can turn almost any leftovers into a fabulous soup, using the formula 1 part onion, 1 part potato, 4 parts any other veggies and enough stock to cover.'

Stuart Gillies

Jay Rayner

Jay Rayner is the *Observer*'s restaurant critic, and an acclaimed food writer and broadcaster. The author of several books, his latest is *The Man Who Ate the World*.

Pork, chorizo and butter bean stew

I adore self-seasoning one-pot dishes, and this stew is a perfect example. Get everything right at the beginning – and it's almost impossible to get it wrong – and it requires almost no care and attention thereafter. Serve with a hunk of warm, crusty bread.

serves 6

6 cooking chorizo sausages (3 spicy and 3 mild can save the stew from blowing your socks off, and make it child friendly)
1 medium onion, chopped
olive oil

1.5kg pork for braising, cut into rough 3cm cubes
400g tin of chopped tomatoes
750ml chicken stock, from cube or powder
400g tin of butter beans

Preheat the oven to 150°C/gas 2. Slice the chorizo into 1.5cm discs, putting a third to one side for later. In a deep casserole dish with a lid, sauté the chopped onion in olive oil until soft. Fry off two-thirds of the chorizo with the softened onion, so that it caramelises and the paprika-rich oil begins to run. When all the chorizo has been cooked, add the pork in handfuls and seal it. It only needs to take on a little colour. As each batch is done, push it to the side to make space for the next until it has all been cooked through and mixed in with the onion and the chorizo.

Add the tomatoes and the stock and mix in until the meat is submerged. Put in the remaining discs of uncooked chorizo and stir in. Bring to a simmer. Strain the butter beans and add them too. Put on the lid, place in the oven, and don't look at it for 2 hours. To check whether the stew is ready, fish out a piece of pork. It should come apart easily when tugged at with a couple of forks. If it's not yet ready, just return to the oven for 20 minutes and check again. If the liquor is a little thin, put the casserole back on the hob without the lid, bring to a gentle boil and reduce the sauce. The stew can easily be prepared ahead of time, and quickly reheated when you need it. Arguably it's even better on day two.

I hate being without Maille Dijon mustard, not for its marvellous properties as a condiment – though I do love it for that – but because of its uses in sauces and gravy. A good teaspoon beaten in both thickens and adds a subtle acidity very efficiently, while also bigging up all the other flavours around it. If we run out I am bereft.

Clive Dixon

Clive Dixon started his career at Le Champignon Sauvage in Cheltenham. He also worked at Cliveden Hotel in Berkshire, and the Mill and Old Swan in Minster Lovell, Oxfordshire. Aged twenty-five he was head chef at Lords of the Manor near Bourton-on-the-Water in Gloucestershire, which got a Michelin star within a year. He is now at the Hinds Head in Bray, Heston Blumenthal's gastropub.

Pheasant pasty

This is a twist on the original Cornish pasty and a lovely way to serve pheasant. The baking time is vital to ensure that the breasts stay moist when cooked in the suet pastry.

serves 4

for the confit pheasant:
80g salt
1 tbs thyme
1 tbs rosemary
1 tbs sage
2 bay leaves
2 cloves of garlic
2g coriander seeds
2g white peppercorns
1 star anise
10 juniper berries
6 cloves
10 cardamom pods
½ a cinnamon stick
the legs and breasts from 2 pheasants (ask your butcher to joint the pheasants for you)
goose fat to cover

for the filling:
30g onions, sliced thinly
50g Alsace bacon
olive oil or goose fat
80g swede, cut into small, thin square slices (*paysanne*)
1 clove of garlic, chopped
150g savoy cabbage, shredded thinly
100g cooked chestnuts, roughly chopped
2 tsp thyme leaves
salt and pepper

for the pastry:
250g self-raising flour
125g suet
7g baking powder
4g salt
150ml ice-cold water
1 egg, beaten

The confit: add the salt to a litre of water and bring it to the boil in a large saucepan, stirring until the salt has dissolved. Blitz all spices and herbs together in a food processor and tie the powder up in a piece of muslin. Remove the water from the heat and add the spice bag to the saucepan. Allow to chill to room temperature. Put the pheasant legs and breasts into the brine and leave for 2 hours, then wash the breasts in cold running water for 30 minutes.

Place the pheasant in a saucepan and cover with goose fat. Cook over a low heat for 5 hours at a very low simmer (approximately 80°C if you have a digital thermometer). After 5 hours, allow to chill in the fat. When cool, pick the meat from the legs but leave the breasts whole. Reserve the fat.

The filling: sweat the onions and Alsace bacon in some olive oil or goose fat from the pheasant. Add the swede and garlic and cook further until the swede becomes lightly coloured. Add the cabbage and stir until it starts to soften, then add the pheasant leg meat, chestnuts and thyme; continue to cook for approximately 15–20 minutes, adding in some of the reserved fat to keep it moist. Remove from the heat when there is no longer any liquid in the bottom of the pan but the mixture is still moist. Add salt and pepper to taste.

The pastry: mix the dry ingredients together in a mixing bowl. Stir in the water a little at a time until it comes together to form a firm dough. Allow to rest for 10 minutes.

To assemble the pasties: preheat the oven to 220°C and place a metal baking sheet on the middle shelf. Divide the pastry into 4 equal balls and, on a floured surface, roll each ball into a circle approximately 17cm wide (3mm thick). Lay a breast in the centre of each circle and put approximately 60g of the filling mix on top of the breast. Wash the edges of the pastry with a little beaten egg and bring them together to join over the filling. Crimp them together with your fingers.

Brush the outside of the pasties with beaten egg. Place the pasties on a piece of baking paper, then transfer them straight on to the hot sheet in the oven. Bake for 12 minutes and serve.

I love oil from Spain, Greece and Italy: they all have different characteristics, so it depends on the dish or even the mood. Beware of Tuscan oil, the peppery heat and rich grassy notes do make it addictive! I've found myself putting it in every soup, stew, egg dishes, etc. Try to buy new season – it's generally harvested in November. Like wine, when opened it will lose its fruity flavour, so use it.

Mark Hix

Haddock fish fingers

These might be a bit more labour-intensive than reaching into the freezer for a packet of fish fingers, but they are far superior. I often serve them with a posh pea purée – made by simply blending a bag of frozen peas to a coarse purée.

serves 4
500g haddock fillet, skinned (you can use pollack or any other firm white fish)
salt and freshly ground black pepper
plain flour for dusting
1 large egg, beaten
100g fresh white breadcrumbs
vegetable or corn oil for frying

Cut the haddock fillet into 8cm x 2cm fingers and season with salt and pepper. Put the flour in one shallow dish, the beaten egg in another and the breadcrumbs in a third dish. One at a time, dip each piece of fish first into the flour, then in the beaten egg and finally into the breadcrumbs to coat all over.

Heat a thin film of oil in a heavy-based frying pan and cook the fish fingers for about 2 minutes on each side until nicely browned.

Drain on kitchen paper and serve straight away, with ketchup and pea purée if you like.

(This recipe is taken from *British Seasonal Food*.)

4 good things to do with parsnips

Mashed parsnips
Mash steamed parsnips with an equal amount of cooked potatoes. Add a little butter and perhaps some milk if you feel it's too thick, and your choice of snipped chives, a couple of tbs plain yoghurt or some wholegrain mustard.

Honey-roast parsnips
Mix a couple of tbs honey with the same of olive oil and wholegrain mustard. Peel and halve your parsnips, place in a roasting tray and toss in the honey mixture. Roast for about 35 minutes.

Spicy parsnip soup
Dry roast 1 tbs cumin seeds in a pan for a couple of minutes, then grind with a pestle. Peel and finely chop 5 parsnips, and do the same to a carrot. Chop an onion. Cook the onion in butter and a touch of olive oil until soft and golden, then add the vegetables. Add the cumin and some dried chilli to taste. Add some finely chopped garlic. Cook until the vegetables are softening. Add stock (chicken or vegetable) to cover, plus about 6cm more, and simmer for 20–30 minutes on a low heat. Blend the soup and add more stock if it's too thick. Add a little cream (optional), season and serve with coriander leaves and Parmesan.

Potato and parsnip rostis
Grate equal amounts of raw, peeled potatoes (squeeze out excess water once grated) and raw peeled parsnips and mix with a large grated onion. Melt 4 or 5 tbs butter and add to the mix with some salt and pepper and thyme leaves. If you like horseradish, add a tbs here too. Shape into flat cakes and fry in butter until golden brown and crispy – 6–7 minutes a side. Finish in the oven for 6–8 minutes to ensure they are completely cooked through. Serve as a side or with a poached egg.

Skye Gyngell

Carrots with honey, lemon zest and thyme

Carrots tend to be a little dull simply boiled, but cooking them with honey and butter gives them a deep caramel flavour, and thyme lends fragrance.

serves 4
8 medium carrots
1½ tbs honey
50g unsalted butter
6 sprigs of thyme
sea salt and freshly ground black pepper
grated zest and juice of ½ a lemon
curly parsley, finely chopped, to sprinkle (optional)

Peel the carrots and cut them into chunky slices on the diagonal. Place in a saucepan and pour on enough cold water to just cover. Add the honey, butter, thyme and a generous pinch of salt. Place over a medium heat and bring to the boil, then lower the heat to a simmer. Cook for 15 minutes or until the carrots are almost tender.

Now, turn the heat up to boil the liquid rapidly until reduced down to a shiny, sweet glaze – there should be 1–2 tbs of intensely flavoured cooking liquor coating the carrots … nothing more. Add the lemon juice and check the seasoning. You'll need a turn of the pepper mill and a pinch or two of salt, but no more.

Just before serving, sprinkle over the lemon zest. A scattering of very finely chopped curly parsley would not go amiss either.

(This recipe is taken from *My Favourite Ingredients*.)

Tristan Welch

Cambridge burnt cream

serves 4
350ml double cream
150ml milk
1 whole nutmeg
6 egg yolks
100g caster sugar, plus extra for the topping

Preheat the oven to 120°C/gas ¹/₂. Pour the milk and cream into a large pan, crush the whole nutmeg into a couple of large pieces and add this too. Cling film the top of the pan and gently bring to a simmer on a low heat, then place to one side to infuse. The cling film helps the infusion.

In a mixing bowl, whisk together the yolks and caster sugar. Gently pour the infusion over the eggs and sugar and mix well.

Pass the custard through a sieve to remove all of the nutmeg. Pour into an ovenproof dish that will hold all the mix (roughly 600ml), making sure the dish is filled right to the top. Place this in a deep oven tray that will allow you to pour 2cm of warm water in the bottom. Bake in the oven for 30–45 minutes, until set. Once the set custard is cooked, allow it to cool (at this stage it can be kept in the fridge for 2 days before serving), then sprinkle over a layer of caster sugar and caramelise with a blowtorch or under the grill. Serve immediately.

Antonin Bonnet

Antonin Bonnet is originally from Lyon and is executive head chef at the Greenhouse in Mayfair. He trained under the three-Michelin-starred chef Michel Bras in Aubac, and has also worked at L'Oustau de Baumanière in Provence. He came to London in 1999 and worked as private chef to restaurateur Marlon Abela as well as at private members' club Morton's. The Greenhouse has one Michelin star.

My grandmother's apple tart

serves 8

for the pastry:
250g flour
a pinch of salt
125g butter
50g caster sugar
1 egg

for the filling:
6 Golden Delicious apples, cored and sliced
50g butter
100g good apricot jam

First you will need to make a shortcrust dough. Mix the flour, salt, butter and 20g of the sugar together until completely crumbly, then add the whole egg and mix until the dough has a smooth texture. Put in the fridge for 1 hour to rest, then roll it into a 24cm tart tin.

Preheat the oven to 200°C–220°C/gas 6–7. Fill the tart case with the sliced apples, brush with some melted butter and sprinkle with the rest of the caster sugar. Cook in the hot oven for about 40 minutes. When the tart comes out, let it rest on a rack so the crust dries out a bit. When cold, brush the apples with a little bit of apricot jam.

Antonin Bonnet

Quick-fix chocolate mousse and hazelnut praline

serves 8

for the praline:
50g whole hazelnuts
25g muscovado sugar
a pinch of Maldon sea salt

for the chocolate mousse:
2g gelatine
150g dark chocolate (65% cocoa solids, at least)
125ml whole milk
250ml single cream, whipped

To make the praline, toast the hazelnuts in a dry pan until dark, then crush them with a pestle and mortar until you get a crumbly sticky texture. Add the sugar and salt and mix. It is now ready.

For the mousse, soak the gelatine in a large bowl of cold water. Chop the chocolate. Bring the milk to the boil and add the gelatine, well drained. Pour around a third of the hot liquid over the chocolate and whip until the texture is smooth, supple and glossy, showing that an emulsion is beginning to form. Add the rest of the milk, making sure the texture stays the same. When still warm, add the whipped single cream and mix gently until frothy. Scatter the praline on top (you can also use this with ice cream or yoghurt, if there's any left). Serve and eat immediately or, for a slightly different pudding, you could freeze it.

My secret ingredient is fresh ginger juice. It really enhances the taste of sauces, a little bit like adding colour to a black-and-white picture.

December

Brussels sprouts, cranberries, parsnips, partridge, rabbit, swede, turnips and venison are all good this month.

Try Giorgio Locatelli's fantastic meatballs using leftover turkey, Anna Hansen's red cabbage, Henry Harris's chestnuts and prunes, or Bryn Williams's bread sauce. Or ignore Christmas and tuck into Atul Kochhar's wonderful chicken curry.

Adam Byatt

Adam Byatt studied at the Académie Culinaire de France for four years and in 1996 competed in the national finals of Young Chef of the Year. He now owns and runs the award-winning Trinity in Clapham, which critics have called 'the perfect restaurant', but before that was head chef and owner of Thyme, also in Clapham and also very popular. His new book is called *How to Eat In*.

Roast partridge with smoked bacon and lentils

serves 4

4 oven-ready red-leg partridges
200g Umbrian grey or puy lentils
1 x 100g piece of smoked pancetta or 100g thinly sliced rashers
1 carrot
2 sticks of celery
½ an onion
600ml white chicken stock
sea salt and freshly ground black pepper
olive oil
50g soft butter
½ a bunch of thyme

Preheat the oven to 200°C/gas 6. Check the partridges for any feathers. If your pancetta is in one piece, trim off any skin and bones and reserve, then slice the pancetta as thin as you can. Drain the soaked lentils and place in a saucepan with the carrot, celery and onion, and any skin and bones from the pancetta. Cover with the stock and bring to the boil, then cook the lentils gently for 45–60 minutes until tender, without allowing them to boil. Set aside to cool.

Season the partridges well with salt and pepper. Put a roasting tray on top of the stove, splash in some olive oil and heat. Place the partridges on their sides in the tray and colour lightly, then repeat on their other sides before turning them on to their backs. Now spread the butter over the birds, and place the thyme sprigs on top. Roast the birds for 15 minutes, carefully basting halfway through cooking. Remove the birds from the oven and leave to rest for at least 10 minutes.

Preheat the grill on a medium setting and grill the pancetta slices gently until crisp. Transfer to paper towels. Remove the vegetables and pancetta trimmings from the lentils, then warm the lentils in the roasting tray on top of the stove. To serve, slice the breasts from the partridges and remove any blood or gristle, then place the breasts on 4 warmed plates. Remove the legs and place under the breasts. Check the seasoning of the lentils and place alongside, then garnish with the crisp pancetta. Serve with a celeriac purée.

Tip: If you find the lentils too rich, add a splash of red wine vinegar or sherry vinegar – it will provide a touch of acidity, which will lighten them.

Atul Kochhar

Atul Kochhar was born in India. At Tamarind in London, he was the first Indian chef to get a Michelin star, when he was thirty-one. He now has his own Michelin-starred restaurant, Benares, in Mayfair, the Colony in Marylebone, and another, Vatika, near Southampton. He has written several books, the latest of which is *Fish Indian Style* and he regularly appears on TV. He often returns to India to research new recipes.

Home-style chicken curry

You can't go wrong cooking this unless you leave the pot on the stove and go on a long vacation. Adding ginger towards the end is a unique step that enhances the flavour. I have cooked this recipe a thousand times – it just keeps getting better.

serves 4

3 tsp vegetable oil
1 bay leaf
4 green cardamom pods, 2.5cm cinnamon stick, 10–12 black peppercorns, 1 tsp cumin seeds, 2 cloves, all pounded together with a pestle and mortar
250g onions, finely sliced
½ tsp garlic, minced to a paste
½ tsp red chilli powder
1 tsp coriander powder
½ tsp turmeric powder
salt to taste
100g tomatoes, roughly chopped
1 tsp tomato purée
600g chicken, boned, cut into 2.5cm dice
½ tsp garam masala
2 tsp coriander leaves, finely chopped
1 tsp ginger, finely chopped

Heat the oil in a pan, add the bay leaf and pounded spices, and stir until the spices crackle and they change colour. Add the onions and sauté until golden brown, then add the garlic paste. Stir continuously and keep scraping the bottom of the pan to avoid burning the mix. Add the red chilli, coriander and turmeric powders. Mix quickly without letting the spices burn. Add salt, the tomatoes and the tomato purée and cook on a slow heat, stirring slowly. As the tomatoes melt to form a sauce, add the chicken and cook on a slow heat for 20–25 minutes until the chicken is almost cooked. Sprinkle on the garam masala and simmer to finish cooking. Add the coriander and sprinkle on the ginger.

Eric Chavot

Potato pie with smoked bacon and crème fraiche

A tasty recipe for these cold days and nights, passed down to me by my father's mother.

serves 6–8

for the sweet shortcrust pastry:
500g plain flour
375g butter
yolks from 3 large eggs
30g caster sugar
15g fine salt
100ml whole milk
1 egg, beaten

for the potato pie filling:
400g crème fraiche
150g double cream
1 sprig of thyme
2 cloves of garlic
salt and pepper
50g unsalted butter
1.5kg peeled and thinly sliced
Charlotte potatoes
250g Alsace bacon, thinly sliced
250g peppered ventrèche (smoked
pork belly), thinly sliced

To make the pastry, place the flour in a bowl, cut the butter into pieces in the bowl and mix with your fingertips until all is combined. Then mix with a paddle in an electric mixer, adding the egg yolks, sugar, salt and milk. Continue until all is homogeneous, without overworking the dough. Cover with cling film and store in the refrigerator, ideally overnight. When rested, roll out and line a roughly 20 x 22 x 6cm deep baking tin or dish, reserving the rest of the dough for the pie lid.

Preheat the oven to 180°C/gas 5. To make the filling, bring the crème fraiche and double cream to a gentle simmer, infuse it with the thyme and garlic, and season with salt and pepper to taste. Whisk the butter into the cream mixture. Lightly season the sliced potato with salt, leave to rest in a colander for 5 minutes and remove the excess water.

Cover the pastry base with 2 to 3 layers of potato, and then a layer of the bacon and ventrèche. Continue until you reach the top of the tin – the top layer should be potatoes. Sieve the cream mixture and pour over the potatoes. Roll out a disc of shortcrust pastry to cover the potatoes, brushing the edge with beaten egg in order to help it stick to the pastry already in the tin. Pinch all the way around the edge of the pie to seal. Make a small X-shape with scissors in the middle of the pie to ensure the steam from the potatoes and cream can evaporate.

Cook in your preheated oven at 190°C/gas 5 for an hour, then turn the oven down to 165°C/gas 3 and cook until the potatoes are soft and tender. When it is ready, the steam coming from the pie should smell slightly smoky from the bacon. Serve immediately with a crunchy green salad with a French dressing and shallots.

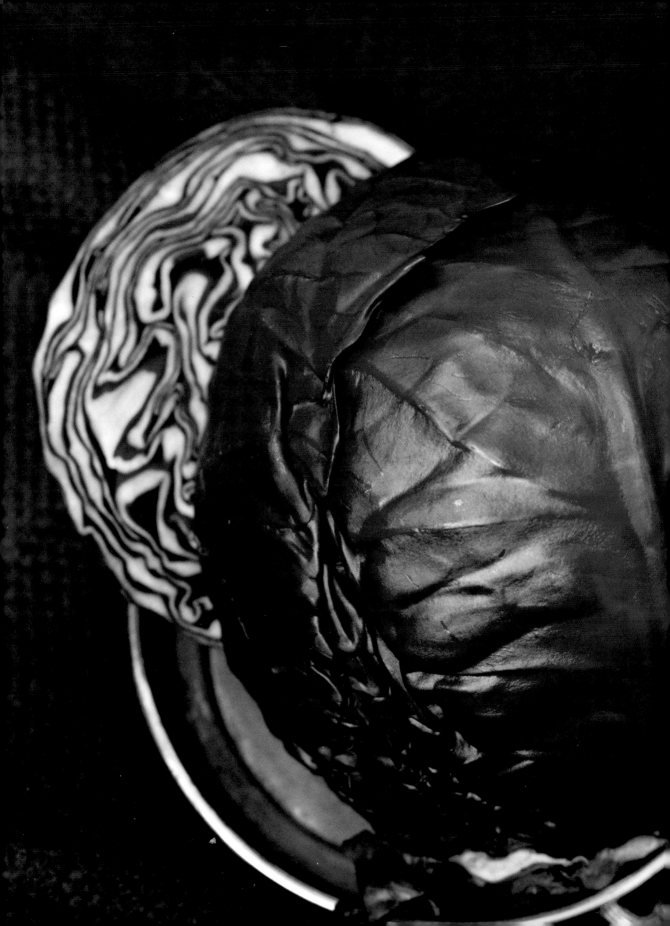

Anna Hansen

Anna Hansen was born in Canada and raised in New Zealand. She trained as a chef under Fergus Henderson, after having studied business management. She went on to open the Providores with Peter Gordon, which won many awards, and left to start the Modern Pantry in London's Clerkenwell in 2008, which already has two AA rosettes.

Braised red cabbage

My mum's side of the family is Danish, which meant lots of pickled herrings, frikadeller (Danish meatballs) and remoulade – a mixture of mayonnaise and piccalilli, which we slathered over innumerable open sandwiches (smørrebrod) – every Christmas. This is my mother's recipe for braised red cabbage. It makes a delicious open sandwich on rye bread with sliced leftover boiled new potatoes and a decent grinding of black pepper.

serves 4–6

1 medium red cabbage, sliced
1 white onion, sliced
zest and juice of 1 small orange
2 Bramley apples, grated with skin on
1 cinnamon stick
1 tbs ground allspice
250ml Cabernet Sauvignon vinegar or good red-wine vinegar
200g soft brown sugar
300ml apple juice

Put all the ingredients into a large heavy-bottomed saucepan and mix thoroughly. Cover with a tight-fitting lid and cook over a medium heat for 5 minutes, then reduce to the lowest setting. Leave to simmer, stirring every 10 minutes or so, for about 30 minutes or until the cabbage is tender. Check the balance of acid to sweet and adjust to your taste.

TRICKS OF THE TRADE

'For perfect cranberry sauce that isn't too sharp,
don't overdo the sugar; instead add the zest and juice
of a very juicy orange.'

Oliver Rowe

Frank Raymond

Frank Raymond is head chef at Mon Plaisir, a restaurant in Covent Garden, London that is reputedly the oldest French restaurant in the city, having been established in the 1940s; Charles de Gaulle ate there in 1942.

Soupe à l'oignon gratinée

serves 2
4 onions, sliced into rings
3 tbs butter
2 tbs flour
500ml stock
6 slices of country bread toasted in the oven
100g grated Abondance cheese

Brown the onion rings in the butter in a non-stick pan. Keep the heat low and stir often so they do not stick. When they start colouring, add the flour and stir for a minute, then add the stock. Cook gently on the hob for 25 minutes.

Butter a small oven dish and line the bottom with 2 slices of toast. Pour some stock on top and a grating of Abondance cheese. Repeat three times, adding a little butter to the last layer. Grill until a fine golden crust forms on the top.

Mitch Tonks

Quick fish soup

serves 3
1 red mullet
1 gurnard
a small handful of mussels
a small handful of clams
1 large or 2 medium onions, finely chopped
2 cloves of garlic, finely chopped
olive oil
a sprig of fresh thyme
a splash of Pernod
a pinch of saffron
3–4 tomatoes, chopped, or a carton of Cirio tomato sauce
fresh parsley, chopped, to serve
salt and pepper

You can pull together a really impressive fish soup in no time if you ask your fishmonger to do some of the work: ask for a red mullet cut into chunks on the bone, a gurnard and a small handful each of mussels and clams. Sweat the onions and garlic in olive oil with the fresh thyme, add the Pernod, a pinch of saffron, the tomatoes (or the Cirio tomato sauce), then the fish, cover with water and simmer for 15–20 minutes. Add the parsley and then season with salt and pepper before serving.

4 good things to do with turkey

Leek and turkey pie
Slice leftover cooked turkey into small pieces. Sweat some sliced leeks in a little butter and mushrooms too, if you fancy – if you've got any baked ham, add some now. Once they are soft, season and add the cooked turkey and heat through. Make a white sauce, enough to cover the meat and vegetables. Pour into a deep pie dish, and cut a sheet of ready-rolled puff pastry just slightly larger than the edge of the dish. Pop it over the pie, press down the edges, cut a couple of vents with a sharp knife, brush with beaten egg and cook in a hot oven for 25 minutes or so, until the pastry is puffed up and the filling bubbling hot. A warming supper for a cold night.

Turkey salad with soy sauce dressing
If you're in need of something raw after Christmas, toss strips of cooked turkey with soy sauce, lime juice and a little sesame or vegetable oil. Then add sliced spring onions, hunks of cucumber, mint, parsley and coriander leaves, some lettuce and even a little red chilli, deseeded and sliced into rings.

Turkey enchiladas
Shred cooked turkey and mix with chopped coriander leaves, chopped red chilli (to taste), raw sliced onion or shallot and grated cheddar cheese. Place a flour tortilla in a hot pan and immediately pile on a layer of the cheese and turkey mix. Squeeze over some lime juice. Put another tortilla on top and allow to cook for a minute or two, until the tortilla is golden and the cheese is beginning to melt. Turn over and allow the other side to brown slightly. Remove from the pan, cut into 8 and squeeze over a little more lime juice. Eat while hot and tasty.

Turkey noodle soup
Fry sliced onions in butter until soft. Add finely chopped cooked turkey and then cover with stock. Add vermicelli or Asian noodles and cook for as long as the packet requires. You can stop here, and serve with Parmesan or cheddar, or add spring onions and coriander leaf and maybe some soy sauce.

Giorgio Locatelli

Turkey meatballs in sweet and sour sauce

serves 4
50g stale country-style bread
2 tbs milk
300g cooked turkey, minced or very finely chopped
200g boiled potatoes, mashed
50g Parmesan, freshly grated
2 small eggs, beaten
1 clove of garlic, crushed
25g parsley, chopped
grated zest of 1 small lemon
sea salt and freshly ground black pepper
100g breadcrumbs
100ml sunflower oil

for the sauce:
200ml olive oil
2 juniper berries
2 bay leaves
2 white onions, thinly sliced
100ml white wine vinegar
50g sultanas, soaked in warm water for 10 minutes, then drained

Cut the crusts from the bread and soak the bread in the milk. Meanwhile, put the turkey in a bowl with the potatoes and mix well. Add the Parmesan, eggs, garlic, parsley and lemon zest, season with salt and pepper and stir well until the mixture comes together. Squeeze out the soaked bread, add to the mixture and stir well. Shape the mixture into 12 small balls with your hands and flatten into mini burgers. Chill for about 30 minutes.

Meanwhile, put the olive oil in a pan with the juniper berries and bay leaves and heat gently. Add the onions and cook for about 20 minutes, until very tender. Add the white wine vinegar and sultanas and cook for 2 minutes. Remove from the heat and leave to cool.

Coat the meatballs in the breadcrumbs. Heat the sunflower oil in a large frying pan, add the meatballs and fry gently for about 5 minutes on each side, until golden and cooked through. Drain on kitchen paper and place on a baking tray. Pour the sauce over the meatballs and leave to infuse for an hour before serving.

Cass Titcombe

Cass Titcombe grew up near Bath, where his parents had a smallholding, and before starting the Canteen chain of restaurants with Dominic Lake and Patrick Clayton-Malone in 2005, worked at Daphne's in London and the Real Food Company in Brighton. There are now several Canteens in London, and their first book, *Great British Food*, was published in 2010.

Canteen bubble and squeak with fried eggs and bacon

We think of bubble and squeak as a way to use up leftovers, but originally it was quite a posh dish made with beef and cabbage. For our version we fry the bubble in meat drippings, and use potatoes that have been roasted in duck fat, to give a delicious savoury meatiness.

serves 4
500g leftover duck-fat roast potatoes
about 150g leftover cooked cabbage or other greens
leftover fat from roast beef, pork or duck
salt and black pepper
12 rashers dry-cure streaky bacon
vegetable oil
8 eggs

Preheat the grill. Coarsely crush the potatoes with your hands. Chop the cooked cabbage. Heat up 2–3 tbs fat in a large frying pan. Add the potatoes and cabbage and cook for 3–4 minutes, mixing well with a wooden spoon. Season with black pepper and salt, if needed. Remove from the pan to a bowl.

Cool the vegetable mix until you can handle it, then divide into four and shape into rounds that are about 8cm in diameter and 3cm thick. A good way to get neat shapes is to use a large pastry cutter or metal ring.

Heat up the frying pan and add a little more fat. Put in the bubble rounds and fry over a medium heat for 3–4 minutes on each side until golden and crisp.

While the bubble rounds are frying, grill the bacon until crisp. When the bubble is ready, keep warm in a low oven. Heat up some vegetable oil in the frying pan on a low heat and cook the eggs until just set. Place the bubble on plates and top each with 3 bacon rashers and 2 eggs.

You can also make this with half roast potatoes and half mash. If you don't have any leftover fat from a roast, use duck or goose fat.

Bryn Williams

Bryn Williams was born in Denbigh, North Wales, where he went hunting and fishing with his family and assumed everyone grew their own food. He trained in Paris and worked at many of London's great restaurants like the Criterion and Le Gavroche. He opened Odette's in London's Primrose Hill with Vince Power in 2006 and is often on programmes like *Great British Menu* and *Saturday Kitchen*.

Bread sauce

This is my take on bread sauce. Even though my mother still cooks the Christmas meal, the bread sauce is my job.

serves 6
500ml milk
½ an onion, in one piece
1 bay leaf
1 clove
50g butter

½ an onion, finely chopped
6 slices of white bread, crusts removed and cut into 2cm squares
a pinch of salt and pepper
nutmeg

Bring the milk to the boil with the ½ onion, bay leaf and clove, and simmer for 2 minutes. In a heavy-bottomed pan melt the butter and chopped onion and cook until soft with no colour. Strain the cooled milk, pour onto the onion and bring to the boil, then remove from the heat and stir in the diced bread. Season with salt, pepper and a grating of nutmeg, cover with a lid, and keep warm until needed.

Henry Harris

Roast shallots, chestnuts and prunes

This is a lovely accompaniment to roast goose or duck at Christmas and is an old family favourite.

serves 4–6
4 tbs duck fat
24 shallots, peeled
salt and pepper

250g peeled chestnuts, the vacuum-packed variety from the supermarket
8 prunes, stoned and halved

Preheat the oven to 180°C/gas 4. Melt the duck fat in an ovenproof dish over a medium flame and then add the shallots. Season with salt and pepper and sauté briskly for 5 minutes or so until the shallots have taken on a nice golden tan. Add the chestnuts, place in the oven and cook for 30 minutes or until the shallots are caramelised and soft. You will need to give the vegetables a turn every 10 minutes to stop them sticking. Throw in the prunes and cook for a further 5 minutes. Transfer to a serving dish.

4 good things to do with sprouts

Sprouts with bacon

Slice sprouts into discs and cook in a little butter for a few minutes. Then add enough vegetable or chicken stock to partially cover and part steam, part poach until the sprouts are tender but not soft – for as little as 5 minutes, probably. Allow the stock to reduce almost completely. Meanwhile, fry some small strips of smoked streaky bacon and crumble them over the sprouts with a grinding of black pepper to serve.

Sprouts with almonds

Simmer sprouts until just tender, then remove, cool slightly and cut in half. Meanwhile, toast some flaked almonds in a dry pan for 30 seconds, until golden and fragrant. Add a little butter to the pan and, when foaming, add the halved sprouts and toss to heat through and coat with the butter. Allow to cook gently for a further couple of minutes.

Sprouts with chestnuts and pancetta

Simmer whole sprouts until just tender – about 5 minutes. In a separate pan, fry lardons of pancetta and when they are crisp add cooked chestnuts (break or chop these into pieces) and heat through. Drain the sprouts and toss them gently in the hot pan, coating them in the fat. Serve with a little chopped parsley stirred through, if you like.

Brussels sprouts with nutmeg

Cook sprouts until tender, then drain and add to a pan of butter. Toss in the butter, then grate over a little nutmeg, some pepper and some Parmesan. Serve.

Philip Howard

Philip Howard is head chef and co-owner of two-Michelin-starred modern-French restaurant the Square in the West End of London, which he set up with Nigel Platts-Martin in 1991. He is also co-owner of the award-winning Ledbury in Notting Hill, and opened Kitchen W8 in Kensington in 2009.

My mum Lynne's mincemeat tart

for the topping:
125g butter
100g sugar
2 tbs vegetable oil (not olive)
1 egg
1 tsp almond essence
250g flour
a pinch of salt
2 tsp baking powder

approx. 400g shortcrust pastry
boozy, homemade mincemeat for the filling
whole almonds, to decorate

To make the topping, cream the butter, sugar and oil, then add the egg and almond essence. Sift in the flour, salt and baking powder and process until it gathers into a ball. Put in the fridge to harden for several hours.

Preheat the oven to 180°C/gas 4. Line a loose-bottomed tart tin with the shortcrust pastry, fill generously with mincemeat (leaving room for the topping) and then grate (using the coarse side of a grater) a layer of topping over the mincemeat. Press down lightly with a fork and make especially sure there are no gaps round the edges. Decorate the top with whole almonds. Cook for about half an hour till slightly risen and browned. Serve warm with crème anglaise, brandy butter, runny cream – whatever you fancy.

A **Knorr chicken stock cube** turns a lacklustre anything into something worth serving!

Claude Bosi

Christmas pudding parfait

serves 8

for the paté à bombe:
225g egg yolks
225ml water
420g sugar

for the parfait:
45g egg whites
20g sugar
300g whipping cream

100g Christmas pudding
180g paté à bombe

Cook the paté à bombe ingredients over a fast simmering bain-marie for 3 hours, whisking occasionally. Transfer to an electric mixer and whisk again until cool. This will make more than the 180g you need for this recipe, but you can use what's left over for other set desserts.

For the parfait, whip the egg whites with the sugar to make a meringue. Whip the cream to form soft peaks. Fold the Christmas pudding with the paté à bombe. Fold in the cream, then fold in the meringue. Pour into eight 8cm-diameter ring moulds or similar. Freeze overnight and, if you like, serve with a sorbet.

I'm enjoying using black garlic at the moment. I love it for its originality and flavour, and you can do things with it that you can't do with regular garlic.

Francesco Mazzei

Francesco Mazzei, from Calabria, learned to cook from his mother and got a job at the age of fourteen in a gelateria in order to buy a pair of Levi jeans. He has worked in Rome, Bangkok and London (at places like Hakkasan, Yauatcha and the Dorchester). He opened L'Anima in the City to rave reviews in 2008, and is working with Pizza Express throughout 2010.

Panettone ripieno

serves 6
1kg panettone

for the mascarpone cream:
100g egg yolks
100g sugar
50g cocoa powder
1 vanilla pod, sliced open and seeds scraped out
350g mascarpone

for the zabaglione cream:
200ml Marsala wine, plus a little extra to wet the panettone
100g egg yolks
100g sugar
30g cornflour
300g mascarpone

for the chocolate glaze:
50ml double cream
150ml milk
225g dark chocolate, chopped
125g milk chocolate, chopped
40g soft butter

For the mascarpone cream: mix the yolks with the sugar, cocoa and vanilla before adding the mascarpone. Mix until smooth.

For the zabaglione cream: boil the Marsala wine, then remove from the heat and allow to cool. In the meantime mix the egg yolks, sugar and cornflour together, then add to the cooled Marsala. Put back on the heat and very gently warm, stirring, to make a custard. Let the mixture cool right down before adding the mascarpone. Beat the mixture until smooth and creamy.

Carefully slice off the rounded top of the panettone without breaking it, and set aside. Cut the remaining panettone into 4 equal round slices and wet each slice with Marsala wine. Take the bottom slice and put a layer of the zabaglione cream across the cut side of the cake, before adding the second slice and layering it with the light mascarpone cream. Repeat the procedure with the other 2 slices before putting the top slice on top. Leave the cake to cool down in the fridge for about 30 minutes.

In the meantime, boil the cream and milk together and remove from the heat. Then add the chopped chocolate and just before serving add the soft butter and mix well. Take the chilled panettone out of the fridge and pour the glaze over the top.

Where to find all the chefs

Tom Aikens

Tom Aikens, 43 Elystan Street, Chelsea, London, 020 7584 2003, www.tomaikens.co.uk; Tom's Kitchen, 27 Cale Street, Chelsea, London, 020 7349 0202, www.tomskitchen.co.uk *Tom Aikens Cooking* (Ebury); *Fish* (Ebury)

Anjum Anand

www.anjumanand.co.uk *Eat Right for Your Body Type* (Quadrille); *Indian Every Day* (Quadrille); *Anjum's New Indian* (Quadrille); *Indian Food Made Easy* (Quadrille)

Jason Atherton

Maze and Maze Grill, 10–13 Grosvenor Square, London, 020 7107 0000, 020 7495 2211, www.gordonramsay.com/maze *Gourmet Food for a Fiver* (Quadrille); *Maze the Cookbook* (Quadrille)

Richard Bertinet

The Bertinet Kitchen, 12 St Andrew's Terrace, Bath, 01225 445531, www.thebertinetkitchen.com *Cook* (Kyle Cathie); *Dough: Simple Contemporary Bread* (Kyle Cathie); *Crust: Bread to Get Your Teeth Into* (Kyle Cathie)

Raymond Blanc

Le Manoir aux Quat' Saisons and Raymond Blanc Cookery School, Church Road, Great Milton, Oxford, 01844 278881, www.manoir.com; www.raymondblanc.com *A Taste of My Life* (Corgi); *Simple French Cookery* (BBC Books); *Raymond Blanc's Foolproof French Cookery* (BBC Books)

April Bloomfield

The Breslin, 20 West 29th Street, New York, +001 212-679-2222, www.thebreslin.com; The Spotted Pig, 314 West 11th Street, @ Greenwich St, New York, +001 212-620-0393, www.thespottedpig.com

Antonin Bonnet

The Greenhouse, 27a Hays Mews, Mayfair, London, 020 7499 3331, www.greenhouserestaurant.co.uk

Claude Bosi

Hibiscus, 29 Maddox Street, London, 020 7629 2999, www.hibiscusrestaurant.co.uk

Adam Byatt

Trinity, 4 The Polygon, Clapham, London, 020 7622 1199, www.trinityrestaurant.co.uk *How to Eat In* (Bantam Press)

Michael Caines

Gidleigh Park, Chagford, Devon, 01647 432 367; the ABode Hotel chain with sites in Exeter, Glasgow, Canterbury, Manchester, Chester, www.abodehotels.co.uk; www.michaelcaines.co.uk

Antonio Carluccio

Antonio Carluccio is no longer a director, but is still involved in the Carluccio's chain of restaurants, www.carluccios.com *Antonio Carluccio's Simple Cooking* (Quadrille); *Antonio Carluccio's Italia* (Quadrille); *Carluccio's Complete Italian Food* (Quadrille); and ten other books

Eric Chavot

Eric Chavot was formerly at the Capital Hotel, London, and is now working on new projects with Pierre Koffmann. Portrait by Suki Dhanda

Samuel and Samantha Clark

Moro, 34–36 Exmouth Market, London, 020 7833 8336, www.moro.co.uk *Moro East* (Ebury); *The Moro Cookbook* (Ebury); *Casa Moro* (Ebury)

Sally Clarke

Clarke's & Clarke's Bread, 122 – 124 Kensington Church Street, London, 020 7221 9225; www.sallyclarke.com
Sally Clarke's Book: Recipes from a Restaurant, Shop and Bakery (Grub Street)

Gennaro Contaldo

Gennaro does cookery courses – go online for details: www.gennarocontaldo.com
Gennaro's Easy Italian (Headline); *Gennaro's Italian Year* (Headline); *Gennaro's Italian Home Cooking* (Headline)
Portrait by David Loftus

Anthony Demetre

Arbutus, 63–64 Frith Street, London, 020 7734 4545, www.arbutusrestaurant.co.uk; Wild Honey, 12 George Street, London, 020 7758 9160

Henry Dimbleby

The LEON chain, all London: Carnaby Street (020 7437 5280); Cannon Street (020 7623 9699); Ludgate Circus (020 7489 1580); Spitalfields (020 7247 4369); Strand (020 7240 3070); Regent Street (020 7495 1514); Bankside (020 7620 0035); Bluewater (01322 427 834); www.leonrestaurants.co.uk
Leon, Book 2: Naturally Fast Food (Conran Octopus)

Clive Dixon

The Hinds Head, High Street, Bray, 01628 626151, www.thehindsheadhotel.com

Alain Ducasse

Alain Ducasse at the Dorchester, Park Lane, London, 020 7629 8866, www.alainducasse-dorchester.com, and worldwide: www.alain-ducasse.com
Grand Livre de Cuisine (Alain Ducasse)
Portrait by Benoît Peverelli

Fuchsia Dunlop

www.fuchsiadunlop.com
Shark's Fin and Sichuan Pepper: A Sweet-sour Memoir of Eating in China (Ebury); *The Revolutionary Chinese Cookbook* (Ebury); *Sichuan Cookery* (Penguin)

Sanjay Dwivedi

Zaika, 1 Kensington High Street, London, W8 5NP, 020 7795 6533

Mark Edwards

Nobu Berkeley St, 15 Berkeley Street, London, 020 7290 9222; Nobu London, 19 Old Park Lane, London, 020 7447 4747; www.noburestaurants.com
Nobu West (Quadrille)

Hugh Fearnley-Whittingstall

River Cottage Stores Ltd, Trinity Square, Axminster, 01297 631862; River Cottage Canteen @ Komedia, 22–23 Westgate Street, Bath, 01225 471578, www.rivercottage.net. Hugh Fearnley-Whittingstall is currently heading the Landshare campaign (http://www.rivercottage.net/landshare), where keen growers are matched with people with land to spare.
River Cottage Every Day (Bloomsbury); *The River Cottage Family Cookbook* (Hodder); *The River Cottage Fish Book* (Bloomsbury); *Hugh Fearlessly Eats It All* (Bloomsbury)
Portrait by Tom Beard

Chris Galvin

Galvin La Chapelle, 35 Spital Square, London, 020 7299 0400; Galvin Café de Luxe, 35 Spital Square, London, 020 7299 0404; Galvin Bistrot de Luxe, 66 Baker Street, London, 020 7935 4007; Galvin at Windows, 28th Floor, 22 Park Lane, London, 020 7208 4021; www.galvinrestaurants.com

Matt Gillan

The Pass at South Lodge, Brighton Road, Nr Horsham, West Sussex, 01403 891711, www.southlodgehotel.co.uk

Stuart Gillies

Boxwood Café, The Berkeley, Wilton Place, Knightsbridge, London, 020 7235 1010; opening soon: the Savoy Grill at The Savoy, the Strand, London; www.gordonramsay.com

COOK

Bill Granger
Bill Granger's restaurants, Bills, are in Australia, in Darlinghurst, Shichirigahama, Woolahra and Surry Hills – for more information: www.bills.com.au
Feed Me Now (Quadrille)

Skye Gyngell
Petersham Nurseries, Church Lane, Off Petersham Road, Richmond, Surrey, 020 8605 3627, www.petershamnurseries.com
My Favourite Ingredients (Quadrille); *A Year in My Kitchen* (Quadrille)

Anna Hansen
The Modern Pantry, 48 Saint John's Square, London, 020 7553 9210, www.themodernpantry.co.uk

Henry Harris
Racine, 239 Brompton Road, London, 020 7584 4477, www.racine-restaurant.com
A Passion for Protein (Key Porter Books); *Harvey Nichols – The Fifth Floor Cookbook* (Fourth Estate)

Sam and Eddie Hart
Quo Vadis Soho, 26–29 Dean Street, London, 020 7437 9585, www.quovadissoho.co.uk; Barrafina, 54 Frith Street, London, 0207 813 8016, www.barrafina.co.uk; Fino Restaurant, 33 Charlotte Street, London, 020 7813 8010, www.finorestaurant.com
Modern Spanish Cooking (Quadrille)

Angela Hartnett
York & Albany, 127–129 Parkway, London, 020 7388 3344; Murano, 20 Queen Street, London, 020 7592 1222; www.gordonramsay.com
Angela Hartnett's Cucina: Three Generations of Italian Family Cooking (Ebury)

Anissa Helou
www.anissas.com
Modern Mezze (Quadrille); *The Fifth Quarter: An Offal Cookbook* (Absolute Press); *Lebanese Cuisine* (Grub Street) and many others

Fergus Henderson
St John Bar & Restaurant Smithfields, 26 St John Street, London; St John Bread and Wine Spitalfields, 94–96 Commercial Street, London; St John Hotel, 1 Leicester Street, London, 020 7251 0848; www.stjohnrestaurant.com
Nose to Tail Eating: A Kind of British Cooking (Bloomsbury); *Beyond Nose to Tail: A Kind of British Cooking, Part II* (Bloomsbury)
Portrait by Laurie Fletcher

Shaun Hill
The Walnut Tree Restaurant, Llanddewi Skirrid, Abergavenny, Monmouthshire, 01873 852797, www.thewalnuttreeinn.com
Better Gravy: and Other Kitchen Secrets (Mitchell Beazley); *How to Cook Better* (Mitchell Beazley); *Cooking at the Merchant House* (Conran Octopus)

Mark Hix
Hix Oyster and Fish House, Cobb Road, Lyme Regis, Dorset, 01297 446 910; Hix Oyster and Chop House, 36–37 Greenhill Rents, Cowcross Street, London, 020 7017 1930; Hix, 66–70, Brewer Street, London, 020 7292 3518; Hix Restaurant and Champagne Bar, Selfridges, 400 Oxford Street, London, 020 7499 5400; www.hixoysterandchophouse.co.uk
British Seasonal Food (Quadrille); *British Regional Food* (Quadrille); *Fish Etc.* (Quadrille); *British Food* (Quadrille)

Simon Hopkinson
Bibendum, Michelin House, London, 020 7581 5817, www.bibendum.co.uk
The Vegetarian Option (Quadrille); *Roast Chicken and Other Stories* (Hyperion); *The Prawn Cocktail Years* (Macmillan); *Gammon and Spinach* (Pan Books); *Roast Chicken and Other Stories – Second Helpings* (Ebury); *Week In Week Out* (Quadrille)

Phil Howard

The Square, 6–10 Bruton Street,
Mayfair, London, 020 7495 7100,
www.squarerestaurant.org;
Kitchen W8, 11–13 Abingdon
Road, London, 020 7937 0120,
www.kitchenw8.com

Tim Hughes

Le Caprice, Arlington Street,
London, 020 7629 2239; The Ivy,
1–5 West Street, London, 020 7836
4751; Scott's, 20 Mount Street,
London, 020 7495 7309; J Sheekey,
28–32 St Martin's Court, 020 7240
2565; and many others, see
www.caprice-holdings.co.uk

David Jones

Momo, 25 Heddon Street, London,
020 7434 4040, www.momoresto.
com

Jacob Kenedy

Bocca Di Lupo, 12 Archer Street,
London, 020 7734 2223,
www.boccadilupo.com
The Geometry of Pasta (Boxtree)

Tom Kitchin

The Kitchin, 78 Commercial Quay,
Leith, Edinburgh, 0131 555 1755,
www.thekitchin.com
*From Nature to Plate: A Seasonal
Journey* (Weidenfeld & Nicolson)

Atul Kochhar

Benares, 12a Berkeley Square
House, London, 020 7629 8886,
www.benaresrestaurant.com; The
Colony, 7–9 Paddington Street,
020 7935 3353; Vatika Restaurant,
Wickham Vineyard, Botley Road,
Shedfield, Southampton, 01329
830405, www.vatikarestaurant.
com; www.atulkochhar.com
Simple Indian (Quadrille); *Fish,
Indian Style* (Absolute Press)

Pierre Koffmann

Recent consultancy has included
a number of major projects,
including London's Bleeding Heart
restaurants group; the English
Beef and Lamb executive; and
specialist work on meat quality
and recipes for organic farmer
and former racing champion Jody
Scheckter.
*Tante Claire: Recipes from
a Master Chef* (Headline);
Memories of Gascony (Pyramid)

Jeremy Lee

Blueprint Café, Design Museum,
Shad Thames, London, 020 7378
7031, www.danddlondon.com

Rowley Leigh

Le Café Anglais, 8 Porchester
Gardens, London, 020 7221 1415,
www.lecafeanglais.co.uk
No Place Like Home (Fourth
Estate)

Giorgio Locatelli

Locanda Locatelli, 8 Seymour
Street, London, 020 7935 9088;
Refettorio, 19 New Bridge Street,
London, 020 7438 8052; Ronda
Locatelli, Atlantis, The Palm,
Dubai
Made in Italy: Food and Stories
(Fourth Estate); *Tony and Giorgio*
(Fourth Estate)

Allegra McEvedy

www.allegramcevedy.com
*Economy Gastronomy: Eat Better
and Spend Less* (Michael Joseph);
Leon: Ingredients and Recipes
(Conran Octopus); *Allegra's
Colour Cookbook* (Kyle Cathie)

Andy Mackenzie

The Avenue at Lainston House
Hotel, Woodman Lane, Sparsholt,
Winchester, Hampshire, 01962
776088, www.exclusivehotels.co.uk

Mourad Mazouz

Sketch (including the Parlour,
Lecture Room, Glade and Gallery),
9 Conduit Street, London, 020 7659
4500, www.sketch.uk.com; Momo,
25 Heddon Street, London, 020
7434 4040, www.momoresto.com

Francesco Mazzei

L'Anima, 1 Snowden Street,
Broadgate West, London, 020 7422
7000, www.lanima.co.uk

Paul Merrett

The Victoria, 10 West Temple
Sheen, East Sheen, London, 020
8876 4238, www.thevictoria.net
Using the Plot (Collins); *Economy
Gastronomy: Eat Better and
Spend Less* (Michael Joseph)

Thomasina Miers

Wahaca: London branches in
Covent Garden (020 7240 1833),
Westfield (020 8749 4517),
Canary Wharf (020 7516 9145),
www.wahaca.co.uk
Mexican Food Made Simple
(Hodder); *Cook: Seasonal Recipes
for Hungry People* (Collins); *The
Wild Gourmets* (Bloomsbury)

Martin Nisbet

Angelus, 4 Bathurst Street,
London, 020 7402 0083,
www.angelusrestaurant.co.uk

Tom Norrington-Davies

Great Queen Street, 32 Great
Queen Street, London,
020 7242 0622
Just Like Mother Used to Make
(Cassell); *Cupboard Love*
(Hodder); *Game* (Absolute Press),
which he co-wrote with his friend
and colleague Trish Hilferty

Tom Oldroyd

Polpo, 41 Beak Street, London,
020 7734 4479, www.polpo.co.uk

Shane Osborn

Pied à Terre, 34 Charlotte Street,
London, 020 7636 1178,
www.pied-a-terre.co.uk
Starters (Quadrille)

Yotam Ottolenghi and Sami Tamimi

The Ottolenghi chain: Notting Hill
(020 7727 1121), Islington (020 7288
1454), Kensington (020 7933 0003),
Belgravia (020 7823 2707),
www.ottolenghi.co.uk
Ottolenghi: The Cookbook (Ebury);
Plenty (Ebury)
Portrait by Richard Learoyd

Oliver Peyton

The National Café, East Wing,
The National Gallery, Trafalgar
Square, London, 020 7747 5942;
The National Dining Rooms,
Sainsbury Wing, The National
Gallery, Trafalgar Square, London,
020 7747 2525; Inn the Park, St
James's Park, London, 020 7451
9999; The Wallace Restaurant,
The Wallace Collection, Hertford
House, Manchester Square,
London, 020 7563 9505; plus the
Peyton and Byrne chain;
www.oliverpeyton.co.uk
The National Cookbook (The
National Gallery)

Gordon Ramsay

Gordon Ramsay Royal Hospital
Road, 68 Royal Hospital Road,
London, 020 7352 4441; Petrus, 1
Kinnerton Street, Knightsbridge,
London, 020 7592 1609, and many
others; www.gordonramsay.com
*Gordon Ramsay's World Kitchen:
Recipes from The F Word*
(Quadrille); *Gordon Ramsay's
Great Escape: 100 of My Favourite
Indian Recipes* (HarperCollins)

Paul Rankin

Cayenne, 7 Ascot House,
Shaftesbury Square,
Belfast, 028 9033 1532,
www.cayenne-restaurant.co.uk
New Irish Cookery (BBC Books);
Gourmet Ireland (BBC Books);
both with Jeanne Rankin

Frank Raymond

Mon Plaisir, 19–21, Monmouth
Street, London, 020 7836 7243,
www.monplaisir.co.uk

Jay Rayner

*The Man Who Ate the World:
In Search of the Perfect Dinner*
(Headline Review); *The Oyster
House Siege* (Atlantic Books);
The Apologist (Atlantic Books)

Simon Rimmer

Greens, 43 Lapwing Lane, West
Didsbury, Manchester, 0161 434
4259, www.greensdidsbury.
co.uk; EARLE, 4 Cecil Road, Hale,
Altrincham, Cheshire, 0161 929
8869, www.earlerestaurant.co.uk
The Accidental Vegetarian
(Mitchell Beazley); *The Seasoned
Vegetarian* (Mitchell Beazley)

Joël Robuchon

Atelier de Joël Robuchon, 13–15
West Street, London, 020 7010
8600, www.joel-robuchon.com
The Complete Robuchon (Grub
Street); *Best of Joël Robuchon*
(Les Éditions Culinaires)

Ruth Rogers and Rose Gray

The River Café, Thames Wharf, Rainville Road, London, 020 7386 4200, www.rivercafe.co.uk
The River Café Classic Italian Cookbook (Michael Joseph); *The River Café Cookbook Easy* (Ebury); *The River Café Pocketbooks* (Ebury); and many others

Michel Roux Jr

Le Gavroche, 43 Upper Brook Street, London, 020 7408 0881, www.le-gavroche.co.uk. Michel Roux is a judge on the BBC's *MasterChef: The Professionals*; *Le Gavroche Cookbook* (Cassell & Co)

Oliver Rowe

Konstam, 2 Acton Street, London, 020 7833 5040, www.konstam.co.uk

Mark Sargeant

The Swan, 35 Swan Street, West Malling, Kent, 01732 521910
Co-author of many of Gordon Ramsay's books
Portrait by John Carey

Vivek Singh

The Cinnamon Club, The Old Westminster Library, 30–32 Great Smith Street, London, 020 7222 2555, www.cinnamonclub.com; Cinnamon Kitchen, 9 Devonshire Square, London, 020 7626 5000, www.cinnamon-kitchen.com
Curry: Classic and Contemporary (Absolute Press); *The Cinnamon Club Cookbook* (Absolute Press); *The Cinnamon Club Seafood Cookbook* (Absolute Press)
Portrait by Cristian Barnett

Matt Tebbutt

The Foxhunter, Nantyderry, Abergavenny, Monmouthshire, 01873 881101, www.thefoxhunter.com
Matt Tebbutt Cooks Country (Mitchell Beazley)

David Thompson

Nahm at the Halkin, The Halkin, Halkin Street, London, 020 7333 1234, www.halkin.como.bz
Thai Food (Pavilion)

Cass Titcombe

Canteen group: Canary Wharf, 40 Canada Square, London; Spitalfields Market, 2 Crispin Place, London; Baker Street, 55 Baker Street, London; Royal Festival Hall, Belvedere Road, London, 0845 686 1122
Canteen: Great British Food (Ebury), with Dominic Lake and Patrick Clayton-Malone
Portrait by Angela Moore

Mitch Tonks

RockFish Grill & Seafood Market, 128 Whiteladies Road, Bristol, 01179 7373784; The Seahorse, 5 South Embankment, Dartmouth, 01803 835147; www.mitchtonks.co.uk
Fish (Pavilion). The recipes in *Cook* are taken from this book and use generally lesser-used species caught in the South Coast fisheries, which are very well managed.
The Aga Seafood Cookbook (Absolute Press); *The Fishmonger's Cookbook* (previously published as *Fresh*, Penguin); *The FishWorks Seafood Café Cookbook* (Absolute Press)
Portrait by Chris Terry

John Torode

Smiths of Smithfield, 67–77 Charterhouse Street, London, 020 7251 7950, www.smithsofsmithfield.co.uk; The LUXE Spitalfields, 109 Commercial Street, London, 020 7101 1751, www.theluxe.co.uk
John Torode's Chicken and Other Birds (Quadrille); *John Torode's Beef and Other Bovine Matters* (Quadrille)
Portrait by Jane Sebire

Giuseppe Turi

Enoteca Turi, 28 Putney High Street, London, 020 8785 4449, www.enotecaturi.com

Andrew Turner

Wiltons, 55 Jermyn Street, London, 020 7629 9955, www.wiltons.co.uk

Valentine Warner

What to Eat Now (Mitchell Beazley); *What to Eat Now – More Please: Spring and Summer* (Mitchell Beazley)
Portrait by Howard Sooley

Tristan Welch

Launceston Place, 1a Launceston Place, London, 020 7937 6912

Bryn Williams

Odette's, 130 Regent's Park Road, London, 020 7586 8569, www.odettesprimrosehill.com

Index

COOK

Acknowledgements

Thanks first to all the chefs who kindly allowed us to reproduce their recipes, and to their assistants and PRs who tirelessly answered all our endless queries and requests. Thanks to Waitrose, who donated a lot of meat, fish and cheese to the recipe-testing and photography process, including the wonderful four-rib of beef on page 54. Thanks to Riverford Organic Veg, who generously gave lots of produce from their veg boxes, including the beautiful lettuce on page 80, roast potatoes on page 4 and beetroot on page 120 (www.riverford.co.uk). Thanks also to Nigel Slater and Jay Rayner, very different but both inspiring food writers, and to another great food writer, Tom Norrington-Davies. For all their help, thanks to Jessica Hopkins, Mia Harris, Patrick Joyce and Sheila Joyce, Martin Parr, Peter Marlow, Jenni Smith, Tom Groves and the Cambria pub in Camberwell. And to all those, past and present, who have been part of *Observer Food Monthly*, especially Nicola Jeal, Caroline Boucher, Louise France, Polly Vernon, Morwenna Ferrier, Eva Wiseman, Nicole Jackson, Jossy Smalley, Leah Jewett, Allan Jenkins and Gareth Grundy, and from the *Observer*, John Mulholland and Jan Thompson. Thanks also to David Eldridge (for his brilliant design) and to Lisa Darnell and Sophie Lazar for being fantastic (and patient).